THE MANIFESTED SONS OF GOD

JOHN FRANCO

www.xulonpress.com

ACKNOWLEDGMENTS

I want to thank the Holy Spirit for inspiring me and allowing me to write this.

I want to thank Janet Haire for the many hours she spent in typing and retyping the manuscript. You're a blessing.

I want to thank my wife of fifty-three years for encouraging me to keep doing it, even when I thought it might be too much for me and for tirelessly editing its entirety.

I want to thank Vickey McCorkle for the inspired painting that adorns the cover of this book. You captured my heart in this.

PREFACE

The Bible says, "The earnest expectation of the creature waiteth for the manifestation of the sons of God" (Romans 8:19 KJV). The New Century Version puts it this way, "Everything God made is waiting with excitement for God to show His children's glory completely. All of the earth is eagerly waiting for the sons of God to display the power that has been given to them."

If you will search within yourself, you will find that within you there is a hunger for the supernatural. Not only to witness it, but also to participate in its performance. This book is designed to help you get out of a sedentary Christian experience into a fruitful walk with God. Signs, wonders, and miracles are within your reach. To be completely upfront with you, right from the beginning, it is what is expected from you. Bear in mind the parable of the talents. The talent that was not invested was taken away and given to the one who used his (Matthew 25:14-29).

When you made Jesus Christ Lord of your life, you became a son of the most high God. His DNA was transferred to you. By having our minds renewed by His Word, we come to know all that is available to us. It is impossible to put into one book all that has been made available to us. I have attempted to give you a good start! This book is intended to be more of a tool than a "read only" experience.

My prayer is that you will allow the contents, all of which is the Word of God, to saturate your being and allow it to change you into what God intends for you.

TABLE OF CONTENTS

1

WHAT?
(I can't say that!)

For with the heart one believes to righteousness and with the mouth confession is made to salvation.

(Romans 10:10 NKJV)

You must read the
first five pages of
this book out loud
in order to get
its full impact.

I thank you Father, that You have given to me the spirit of wisdom and revelation in the knowledge of You. Thank You that the eyes of my understanding are enlightened. I know what is the hope of Your calling. I know what the riches of the glory of Your inheritance are in me, a Saint. I know what is the exceeding greatness of Your power towards me as a believer. It is heavenly Father, according to the working of Your mighty power which You worked in Christ when You raised Him from the dead, and You seated Him at Your right hand in the heavenly places.

I thank You, that You have granted me, according to the riches of Your glory, to be strengthened with might through Your Spirit in the inner man. Christ dwells in my heart through faith, I am rooted and grounded in love, I am able to comprehend with all the saints what is the width and the length, the depth, and the height. I know the love of Christ which passes knowledge. I am filled with all the fullness of God.

I thank You Father, that my love abounds still more and more in knowledge and all discernment; that I approve the things that are excellent; that I am sincere and without offense until the day of Christ. I am filled with the fruit of righteousness which are, by Jesus Christ, to the glory and praise of You.

I thank You Father, that I am filled with the knowledge of Your will in all wisdom and spiritual understanding. I do have a walk worthy of You Lord. I fully please You, I am fruitful in every good work, and I am increasing in the knowledge of You. I am strengthened with all might according to Your glorious power for all patience and long-suffering with joy. I give thanks to You Father for You have qualified me to be a partaker of the inheritance of the saints in the light. You, Heavenly Father, have delivered me from the power of darkness. You have translated me into the kingdom of the Son of Your love, in whom I have redemption through His blood, the forgiveness of sins. For in Him dwells all the fullness of the Godhead bodily; in whom are hidden all the treasures of wisdom and knowledge. I am complete in Him, who is the head of all principality and power.

I thank You Father, that You make me increase and abound in love towards everyone, so that You may establish my heart blameless in holiness before You at the coming of the Lord Jesus Christ with all His saints. I thank You, Father, that You count me worthy of my calling. I am thankful that You fulfill all the good pleasure of Your goodness and the work of faith with power that the name of my Lord Jesus Christ, is now being glorified in me and I in Him, according to Your grace.

Grace to me and peace from God my Father and the Lord Jesus Christ. Blessed be the God and Father of my Lord Jesus Christ, who has already blessed me with every spiritual blessing in the heavenly places in Christ, just as He chose me in Him, before the foundation of the world, that I should be holy and without blame before Him in love. He has predestined me to adoption as a son, by Jesus Christ to Himself, according to His good pleasure, to the praise of the glory of His grace, by which He has made me accepted in the beloved.

In Him I have redemption through His blood, the forgiveness of sins, according to the riches of His grace, which He made to abound towards me in all wisdom and prudence. He has made known to me the mystery of His Will, according to His good pleasure which He purposed in Himself; that in the dispensation of the fullness of the times He might gather together in one, all things in Christ, both which are in heaven and which are on earth in Him. In whom also I have obtained an inheritance, having been predestined according to the purpose of Him who works all things according to the counsel of His will that I, who first trusted in Christ, should be to the praise of His glory.

He made me alive who was dead in trespasses and sins, in which I once walked according to the course of this world, according to the prince of the power of the air. The Spirit who now works in the sons of disobedience, among whom also I once conducted myself in the lusts of my flesh, fulfilling the desires of the flesh and of the mind. I was by nature a child of wrath just as the others, but God, who is rich in mercy because of His great love with which He loved me even when I was dead in trespasses, has made me alive together with Christ. He has raised me up together and made me sit together in the heavenly places in Christ Jesus, that in the ages to come He might show the exceeding riches of His grace in His kindness towards me in Christ Jesus.

For by grace, I have been saved through faith and that not of myself. It is the gift of God, not of works, lest I should boast. For I am His workmanship, I have been created in Christ Jesus for good works, which God the Father has already prepared beforehand that I should walk in them.

I was once a Gentile in the flesh and at that time I was without Christ. I was an alien from the commonwealth of Israel, and I was a stranger from the covenants of promise.

I had no hope and I was without God in the world. But now, in Christ Jesus, I who was once far-off have been made near by the blood of Christ; for He Himself is my peace, who has made both one and has broken down the middle wall of division between us. He has abolished in His flesh the enmity, that is the law of commandments contained in ordinances, so as to create in Himself one new man from the two, thus making peace that He might reconcile them both to God in one body through the Cross. He has thereby put to death that enmity.

He came and preached peace to me who was far-off and to those who were near. For through Him I now have access by one Spirit to the Father. Now, therefore, I am no longer a stranger and a foreigner, but I am a fellow citizen with the saints and a member of the household of God. I have been built on the foundation of the apostles and the prophets. Jesus Christ Himself is the chief cornerstone in whom the whole building, being joined together, grows into a holy temple in the Lord, in whom I also am being built together for habitation of God in the Spirit.

I dwell in the secret place of the most high. I abide under the shadow of the Almighty. I say of You Lord, "Lord, You are my strength and my fortress, You are my God, My Lord; in You and only in You do I trust." Surely You have delivered me from the snare of the fowler and from the perilous pestilence. You have covered me with Your feathers and under Your wings I do take refuge. Your truth, Heavenly Father, is my shield and it is my buckler. I am not afraid of the terror by night, nor of the arrow that flies by day, nor of the pestilence that walks in darkness, nor of the destruction that lays waste at noonday. One thousand may fall at my side and ten thousand at my right hand, but it shall not come near me. Only with my eyes shall I look and see the reward of the wicked.

Since I have made the Lord even the most high, my refuge and my habitation, no evil befalls me nor does any plague come near my dwelling. You have given Your angels charge over me to keep me in all my ways. They do bear me up in their hands lest I dash my foot against a stone. I tread upon the lion and the cobra and I trample them underfoot.

"Because he has set his love upon Me," saith the Lord, "I will deliver him; I will set him on high because he has known My name." "He shall call upon Me," saith the Lord, "and I will answer him. I will be with him in trouble; I will deliver him and honor him. With long life I will satisfy him and show him My salvation!" Thank You, Lord.

You may be saying to yourself, "How can I say these things? They are not really true. I could only wish they were so." You **can** and you **must** say them. This is how God sees you and this is what you became after accepting Jesus as your Lord and Savior. As far as God is concerned, He chose you in Christ Jesus before the foundation of the world, to be holy and without blame before Him. Now it becomes your responsibility to accept all that God has provided for you, and to no longer be conformed to this world, but become transformed by the renewing of your mind.

This is all based on three scriptural principals from the Word of God:

1. Jesus says, "You can have what you say" (Mark 11:22-24).
2. Corinthians 4:13 says, "If we believe we will speak."
3. You can "call things which be not as though they were" (Romans 4:17).

Based upon these three scriptural principals, you can say these things and you **must** say them for them to become manifested in your life. Remember God already sees you this way; **you want it to become real in you!**

Everything that Jesus did during His earthly ministry was done as a man dependent on His heavenly Father and the Holy Spirit which He received at the Jordan River when He submitted to baptism by John the Baptist. Jesus did absolutely nothing as God or as the Son of God. The Bible says, "He made himself of no reputation, taking the form of a servant and coming in the likeness of men" (Philippians 2:7). My margin says, He emptied Himself of His privileges. Therefore, He came as a man and everything He did, He did as a man.

Then He sent us into the world even as the Father (the same way) sent Him into the world. He also said, "The glory that you have given me, Father, I have given them" (John 17:22). Just before He was taken up, He said, "All authority has been given to me in heaven and on earth, go therefore," (Matthew 28:18) in essence, transferring that authority which He received to whosoever will.

Authority is transferable. Jesus transferred His authority to His twelve disciples in Luke chapter nine, then to seventy others in Luke chapter ten, and they came back rejoicing that even the demons were subject to them in His name. However, the thing that I want to focus on is what Jesus said in John 14:12, "Most assuredly I say to you, he who believes in Me, The works that I do, he will do also; and greater works than these he will do because I go to My Father."

So how do we get from where we are now to the place that Jesus expects us to be? In the fourth chapter of the Gospel of Mark, Jesus likened the Word of God to seeds. Then, in the twentieth verse, He declares, "when the Word of God is planted in good ground, you can expect at least a thirty fold harvest and as much as sixty or even one hundred fold." The important thing to understand here is that God's Words are seeds and they will produce a harvest.

All of the confessions in the pages of this book are confessions that I have made and continue to make daily. The confessions that are on the first four pages of this book are from Ephesians chapters one and three. I have put them in the first person, changing "you and us" to "I and me. " The next two pages after that are prayers written by Paul. I have also put Psalm 91 in the first person.

If you declare something for the future, it will always remain in the future since we never exist in tomorrow, we always exist in today. This is what the Holy Spirit says, "Today, if you will hear His voice," (Hebrews 4:7), never tomorrow. Now there is that other question some may say,

"How can I say these things about myself when they are not true?" Because **God sees you that way already!** Since we are the Body of Christ, He expects it to not only be a positional truth you are in by the grace of God, but He expects it to become an experiential truth for you. It is the way to experience what God has provided for you. You must adhere to the three principles that have been previously mentioned.

The Bible is replete with examples of our free will, commencing with man's very first act of his will in the very beginning of the book of Genesis. You will remember when Adam ate the forbidden fruit against God's will. Adam's will was done, not God's. Not only that, but God did not step in and violate Adam's will.

God has given humanity a free will to do whatever they choose to do, and He will never violate their will. If you would be honest with yourself and reflect on your life, I am certain that you'll remember at least one time when you chose to do what you wanted knowing that it violated God's will. Yet God did not step in and interfere because He will not violate your will.

In Deuteronomy 30:19, God says, "I call heaven and earth as witnesses against you, that I have set before you life and death, blessing and cursing, therefore; choose life that both you and your descendants might live." You will notice that God said, "You choose." Further, you will notice God helps you to make the right decision, but still leaves the choice up to you. You have a free will to do whatever you choose to do.

When you made the decision to accept Jesus Christ as your Lord and Savior, it was your decision. Many Christians have never made the decision to grow up spiritually and become what God intended. It is a choice you make; it does not come automatically. Many say I am a Christian, I expect all these things to come to me. However, they never do come and they never do anything about it. No choice has been made.

You may say to me, "Actually, I have made a decision to begin to grow spiritually but every time I begin to do so, the devil hinders me and I'm not able to."

You are believing a lie! Satan cannot stop you from making the decision that you want to make. Do you remember the Gadarene Demoniac? The Bible does not tell us how many demons were in him. However, it does tell us that Jesus cast them out of him and into two thousand swine. Yet they were not able to stop the man from falling down before Jesus and worshipping Him. Can you imagine more than two thousand demons could not stop him from worshipping Jesus (Mark 5:6).

Do not believe the lies of the enemy. Choose to believe the truth of God's Word. "I can do all things through Christ who strengthens me" (Philippians 4:13). As long as you continue to listen to the lies of the enemy, you will never succeed. However, if you choose God's Word over all circumstances, you will succeed.

In Joshua 1:8 God tells us:

1. If you meditate on His Word;
2. Keep that Word in your mouth;
3. Then you will understand to do it;
4. Then you will bring to yourself prosperity;
5. Then you will have good success.

Romans 10:10 says, "It is with the mouth (using words) that I confess everything that God wants me to be." The reason that I am saved is because I confessed with my mouth (using words) that Jesus Christ is Lord. Then with my mouth, I asked Jesus to become Lord of my life. For many Christians, confessing stops at the altar for salvation (born again). With others, there is some confession made for healing, and still others may make some confessions for prosperity. But what are we doing to become what God intended for us to be!

In Ephesians chapter one, we are told that God chose us (the born again believer) so that:

1. We should be holy and without blame before Him in love.
2. He predestined us to adoption as sons.
3. He made us accepted in the beloved.
4. We have redemption through His blood.
5. We have forgiveness of sins by His grace.
6. We have obtained an inheritance.

I remember reading this scripture years ago and thinking, "Someday in the sweet by and by, this will all come to pass." However, since then I have come to realize this is all true **now**! We put it off into the future by not acting on it. I was born into a Christian family. My father was a preacher. I had heard all these things since I was a child. Yet, I knew beyond a shadow of a doubt that I was not experiencing any of this. Was it within my grasp? Could I really become what the Word said that I was? Did I have to wait until I got to heaven to experience it? As far as God is concerned it is true **now**. It became a reality when I accepted Jesus as my Lord and Savior.

Positionally, you are whatever the Word says you are. You became righteous at the new birth. When God looks at you, you have become a member of the Body of Christ and that's what He sees. "Therefore, if anyone is in Christ, he is a new creation, old things have passed away; behold all things have become new" (2 Corinthians 5:17). The words, "passed away," mean the same thing in the Bible as it does in newspapers. Your old unregenerate spirit has passed away and you became a new creation. That is what it says in Ezekiel 36:26, "I will give you a new heart and put a new spirit within you: I will take the heart of stone out of your flesh and give you a heart of flesh."

However, you may not be experiencing what God made you because you haven't made a decision to:

1. Believe what God says about you.
2. Accept by faith what you are and what God says you are.

Let's go back again to Romans 10, "With the mouth (words spoken) confession is made unto salvation." Therefore, everything that God has must be received. Furthermore, we are told, "I believed, therefore I spoke" (Psalm 116:10). If we truly believe what God says about us we will speak it out of our mouths in faith. Paul tells us, "But since we have the same spirit of faith, according to what is written, I believed and therefore, I spoke; we also believe and therefore speak" (2 Corinthians 4:13).

When you study the Word of God, your mind is being renewed and your old thought patterns begin to be replaced by what God says. It is not until you begin to confess what the Word says you are from your mouth that you begin to experience it in reality. You were what the Word said you were positionally; God saw you that way. By beginning to speak it out of your mouth, you begin to see yourself that way, and it becomes a reality in your life.

I AM NOT TRYING TO
DEFEAT SATAN. HE
HAS BEEN DEFEATED
ALREADY BY MY LORD
JESUS CHRIST. ALL I AM
DOING IS MAINTAINING
THE DEFEAT THAT
JESUS HANDED HIM.

2

POWER

But you shall receive power when the
Holy Spirit has come upon you.

(Acts 1:8 NKJV)

P aul admonished that, "in the last days perilous times would come that men would have a form of godliness but denying its power" (2 Thessalonians 3:5). Denying does not necessarily mean that people say, "No, there is no power."

You could be denying God's power by:

1. Not pursuing it.
2. Not making a quality decision to understand it.
3. Not accepting what it truly is.

That is exactly what has happened, especially here in America; we have not made a distinct quality decision to understand and know the power of God.

Acts 1:8 reads, "But you shall receive power when the Holy Spirit is come upon you; and you shall be witnesses to me in Jerusalem and in all Judea and Samaria and to the ends of the earth." Any time I have ever heard anyone preach on this verse, it has always been that the power is to live a Christian life. While that is true, it is only part of the truth. Luke wrote the book of Acts, but he also wrote the Gospel of Luke. In the Gospel of Luke, he wrote the account to "Most Excellent Theophilus" (Luke 1:3). He opens the Acts of the Apostles by saying, "The former account I made, O Theophilus, of all that Jesus began both to do and teach" (Acts 1:1). Therefore, to truly understand what Luke was saying in Acts 1:8, we need to examine the gospel of Luke to see if there are any clues there.

I doubt very seriously if Luke knew his writings would end up in the Bible. The only Bible they had in Luke's day was what we today call the Old Testament. It wasn't until the year 1450 that the first Bible with both the Old and New Testaments went into print. Therefore, I believe his writings, in his mind, were for his present-day reader and not for future readers.

We will begin by looking at Luke chapter twenty-four. Remember that two disciples were on the road to Emmaus. They were dejected and sad as they were speaking of things that had taken place in Jerusalem. While they were walking and talking, Jesus came to them and said, "What kind of conversation is that that you have with one another as you walk and are so sad?" (Luke 24:17). They retorted, "Are you the only stranger in Jerusalem and have you not known the things which have happened there in these days?" (Luke 24:18). Jesus, not wanting to reveal Himself to them, answered, "What things?" (Luke 24:19). They replied, "The things concerning Jesus of Nazareth." Finally, Jesus said to them, "O foolish ones and slow of heart to believe in all that the prophets have spoken! Ought not the Christ to have suffered these things and to enter into His Glory?" (Luke 24:25-26). After expounding to them all the scriptures concerning Himself, He vanished from their sight.

They immediately returned to Jerusalem to the eleven disciples and told them the things that had happened on the road. As they were speaking, Jesus Himself appeared in their midst saying, "Peace to you" (Luke 24:36). He spoke at length with them, explaining certain things to them and ended with this statement, "and you are witnesses to these things" (Luke

24:48). The only people that could be "witnesses to these things" were the ones present as He said it.

Notice Jesus continued by saying in verse forty-nine, "Behold, I send the promise of my Father upon you; but tarry in the city of Jerusalem until you are endued with **power** from on high" (Luke 24:49 emphasis added). That power that Jesus was talking about was and is the same power that He operated in on this earth. You will notice that Acts 10:38 states that God anointed Jesus with the Holy Spirit and with **power**. Since there is no recorded evidence in the New Testament that God separately anointed Jesus with **power**, then it is safe to believe He received **power** together with the Holy Spirit in the Jordan River. Jesus said, "Behold, I send the promise of My Father upon you; but tarry in the city of Jerusalem until you are endued with **power** from on high."

I personally believe that the enemy has pulled the wool over the Body of Christ's eyes so that this went unnoticed, rendering the Body of Christ powerless. Now, if what I am saying is correct, then we **must** find proof of this in the New Testament. Let's peruse the Bible and find out.

Let's begin in Acts 2:1-4 with the day of Pentecost. "Now when the day of Pentecost had fully come, they were all with one accord in one place. Suddenly there came a sound from heaven, as a mighty rushing wind, and it filled the whole house where they were sitting. Then there appeared to them, divided tongues, as fire and one sat upon each of them. They were all filled with the Holy Spirit and began to speak with other tongues as the Spirit gave them utterance." You will notice that it says they were all filled with the Holy Spirit, but it says nothing about power. When the Holy Spirit descended upon Jesus, there was no mention of power either. However, at His first show of power, turning water into wine, it became apparent. So it would also be with the disciples. They would be mocked by the crowd for speaking in tongues, but Peter stood up with the eleven. What followed was the very first act of **power** by the disciples in the New Testament. It was so powerful that three thousand souls were added to them (Acts 2:41). This was a definite demonstration of power.

The very next demonstration of power comes in Acts 3 as Peter and John are going to the temple to pray. There was a lame beggar at the gate of the temple who sees Peter and John approaching and he asked for alms. Now watch this demonstration of power unfolding. Peter says to him, "Look on us." But wait Peter, we have been taught to say, "Look on Jesus" not on us. Peter had received power and knew it. That got the beggar's attention so that Peter could give him a miracle. Next, it says, "I don't have any loose change on me right now." Do you really believe that Peter was poor? He was in the fishing business.

What followed is the most amazing part. Peter goes on to say, **"But what I do have I give you"** (Acts 3:6). What we would say today, "But I do have something and I am going to give it to you." Those are words of **power** not words of a power-less man. If you said those words in some churches today, they would kick you out saying, "Only God has power, not you."

Without hesitation Peter bent down, took the man by the hand and said, "In the name of Jesus Christ of Nazareth, rise up and walk." Peter pulled the lame man to his feet and the man began to walk. I, personally, believe that is a great demonstration of God's power. Please remember that Jesus said, "The Father who dwells in me does the works" (John 14:?16). I am sure if you had the opportunity to ask Peter, he would say, "The Father in me, He does the works."

In Acts 4:4, we are told that five thousand men became believers because of this display of the **power** of God. The high priest, elders, and scribes asked Peter and John, "By what **power** or by what **name** have you done this?" (Acts 4:7 emphasis added). This indicated that they recognized the show of power. Later on they called the incident "a notable miracle" (Acts 4:1).

If there were **notable miracles** happening here in America, I believe it would silence the liberal press. However, I believe that in the coming days there will be many taking place and they will not be able to dispute it. In Acts 4:3 we are told, "With great **power** the apostles gave witness to the resurrection of the Lord Jesus Christ" (emphasis added). Then in Acts 6:8 it tells us that Stephen was full of faith and **power**. When and how did Stephen get this power? Is God a respecter of persons? No, absolutely not! Stephen got it on the day of Pentecost in the upper room.

Now I am going to point out to you something that may turn you off and tempt you to put this book down. Remember God's Word is **truth**. There is no greater or any other truth but the Word of God. There may be facts, but the truth will always triumph over facts. The Holy Spirit gives credit for miracles, healings, signs, and wonders to the person who listens to the Word of God and obeys it. In Acts 8:5-7 we are told, "Then Philip went down to Samaria and preached Christ to them." It doesn't say he witnessed it says, "He preached Christ to them." Jesus said before His Ascension, "Go into all the world and preach the Gospel" (Mark 16:15). In Acts 8:6 it continues saying, "And the multitudes, with one accord, heeded the things spoken by Philip; hearing and seeing the miracles which **he did**" (emphasis added). We are also told that Paul prayed and laid hands on Publius' father on the Island of Malta. Scripture says, "He (Paul), laid hands on him and healed him" (Acts 28:8). It is correct to say Paul laid hands on him and Paul healed him.

When the man in Lystra was listening to Paul preach, Paul said with a loud voice, **"Stand up straight on your feet."** We are told in the Acts 4:11, "Now when the people saw what Paul had done, the Holy Spirit, through Luke, gave Paul credit for the healing. You may say, "Only God can heal." My answer to you is, "You are absolutely right." Let me say it again together with you, **"Only God can heal."** Let me ask you this, "If Paul was not on that island, would the man have been healed? If Paul ignored the man and did not pray for him, would the man be healed? If Philip had not gone to Samaria, would those miracles have occurred?" The answer to those questions is an astounding, "No!"

Let me tell you what Jesus said, "The words that I speak to you, I do not speak on my own authority but the Father who dwells in me does the **works**" (John 14:10b emphasis added). However, in the same chapter and only two verses later He says, "Most assuredly, I say to you, he who believes in me, the works that I do he will do also" (John 14:12). Is Jesus contradicting Himself? Absolutely not! He expects us to understand that although it is the Father whose power performs, He cannot perform without you or me. That is what is meant by, "We are the hands, feet, and mouth of Jesus." It is time to put down all false humility and begin to declare, "I can do all things through the anointing that empowers me."

However, that is not enough. I believe we must have more evidence from the Word of God to establish that we have been given power after the Holy Ghost is come upon us. Let's examine Paul's ministry and writings.

And I, brethren, when I came to you, I did not come with excellence of speech or of wisdom declaring to you the testimony of God. For I determined not to know anything among you except Jesus Christ and Him crucified. I was with you in weakness, in fear and *in much trembling, and my speech and my preaching were not with persuasive words of human wisdom, but, in demonstration of the Spirit and **power** that your faith should not be in the wisdom of men but in the **power** of God. (1 Corinthians 2:1-5 emphasis added)*

Paul was a very brilliant man and he could have used words to make himself look and sound important, but that is not what he was interested in. His concern was to edify, uplift, and teach the Corinthians truth. Instead of majoring on his speech and preaching, he majored on something else. He said, "My speech and my preaching were not with persuasive words of human wisdom, **but** in demonstration of the Spirit and of **power**." You could say it this way, "I demonstrated God's power." What was his purpose for demonstrating the power of God? It was to show that "your faith should not be in the wisdom of men but in the power of God" (1 Corinthians 2:5). Sadly, many Christians' faith does depend on the wisdom of man.

Many preachers study heavily in order to speak masterfully and to show how much they know, but where is God's **power**? Paul reiterated this in 1 Thessalonians 1:5, "For our gospel did not come to you in word only, but also in **power**." However, the most surprising thing that I have found in scripture is in 1 Corinthians 4:19-20 that says, "But I will come to you shortly, if the Lord wills and I will know, not the word of those who are puffed up, **but the power.** For the Kingdom of God is not in word but in **power**" (emphasis added). Where is this power, then? Has God changed? No, a thousand times, no! You received that power when you were baptized in the Holy Ghost. However, "My people perish for lack of knowledge" (Hosea 4:6).

Let's talk about authority for a moment. Authority is transferable. However, the person to whom authority is being transferred to must be willing to accept it. "Jesus gave the disciples authority over all demons and to cure diseases" (Luke 9:1). In Luke 10 Jesus gave the seventy the same authority. The Body of Christ has fallen short in this area. They think, "If God tells me to do something, I will obey."

The three major areas where the church has missed it are:

1. **Waiting on God** – God is always in the "on" position; He never sleeps nor slumbers. He has given us His Word, which becomes our authority to do what it says to do. There is no need to be waiting on God; truth be said, God is waiting on you. He told Moses in Exodus 14:1, "Why do you cry to Me? Tell the children of Israel to go forward; but, lift up your rod and stretch out your hand over the sea and divide it." In reality He was telling Moses, "You divide, don't wait on Me, you do something." God hasn't changed.

2. **Asking God to do what He has already done** – If God has already done something don't ask Him to do it; instead accept it as a done deal. That is why this book begins with Ephesians Chapters 1 and 2, putting it into the now and first person.

3. **Asking God to do for us what He said we must do** – God tells us to do certain things such as in Romans 12:2, "Do not be conformed to this world, but be transformed by the renewing of your mind." If you want transformation in your life, you must renew your **mind** or else transformation will never come. Don't ask God to do for you what He has told you to do.

Jesus spoke to some five hundred disciples just before His departure from this earth to be seated at the right hand of Majesty, on what we call the Mount of Ascension. I'm sure you will agree with me that since He was leaving, He would have wanted to tell them the most important things that He wanted them to know. For many years I wondered why He did not say something about His name such as: a name has been given to Me that is above all names, so take My name and conquer the world. But He did not touch this subject at all. In my estimation He spoke what is one of the most important things that the Body of Christ needs to know in Matthew 28:18-19, "**All authority** has been given to Me in heaven and earth. **Go ye therefore**, and make disciples of all nations" (emphasis added). His words transferred His authority to those disciples and all who would become disciples through them. You see authority is transferable.

Now authority that seeks to be transferred is either refused or received and accepted. Remember, everything God has must be received. God will not force anything upon you, especially authority.

You will never do anything until:

1. You see yourself doing it (visions and dreams).
2. You speak it out of your mouth; only then will it become a reality.

THE NEXT FIVE PAGES ARE CONFESSIONS TO MAKE CONCERNING POWER.

I arise and I shine for my light has come and the glory of the Lord has risen upon me, darkness covers the earth and thick darkness is over the people, but You, Lord, You arise over me and Your Glory, it appears over me, nations will come to my light and kings to the brightness of my dawn (Isaiah 60:1-3).

I have been conformed to the image of God's son that He might be the firstborn among many brethren (Romans 8:29).

I do go about doing good works because Jesus said, "The works that I do shall you do also, and greater works than these you will do because I go to My Father." Also, I am His workmanship; I have been created in Christ Jesus for good works which the Father has already prepared beforehand that I should walk in them. I am a doer of the Word of God and not a hearer only (John 14:12, Ephesians 2:10).

I cast down imaginations and every high thing that exalts itself against the knowledge of God and I bring into captivity every thought to the obedience of Christ (2 Corinthians 10:3-5).

I let my light so shine before men that they may see my good works and glorify my Father in heaven (Matthew 5:16).

The Father in me, He does the works (John 14:10).

The Spirit of the Lord is upon me because He has anointed me to preach the Gospel (Luke 4:18).

God has anointed me with the Holy Ghost and with power, so that I can go about doing good and healing all those who are oppressed of the devil because God is with me (Acts 10:38).

Thank You Father that, when I preach, I do so not with persuasive words of man's wisdom, but in demonstration of the Spirit and of power, that the hearers' faith should not rest on the wisdom of man but the power of God. For the Kingdom of God is not in word but in power (1 Corinthians 2:1, 4:20).

For the Gospel should not go forth in word only, but also in power and in the Holy Spirit and in much assurance (1 Thessalonians 1:5).

Your Word in my mouth Father is as a fire and as a hammer that breaks the rock in pieces (Jeremiah 23:29).

Lord, I thank You that with all boldness I speak Your Word and You stretch out Your hand to heal; that signs and wonders are done through the name of Your Holy Servant, Jesus (Acts 4:29-30).

I shall decree a thing and it will be established unto me (Job 23:28).

Through God, I am doing valiantly for it is He who treads down my enemies (Psalm 108:13).

Here in is my Father glorified, that I bear much fruit (John 15:8).

I am not slothful, but I am a follower of them who, through faith and patience, inherit the promises (Hebrews 6:12).

All of the promises of God are yea and amen and all of the promises of God are mine; therefore, I am standing on the promises of God (2 Corinthians 1:20).

I have received abundance of grace and I have been given the gift of righteousness; as a result, I am now reigning in life as a king by Jesus Christ (Romans 5:17).

I have no veil over my face, therefore, I am a mirror that brightly reflects the glory of the Lord; as the Spirit of the Lord works in me, I become more and more like Him (2 Corinthians 3:18 TLB).

I have been born of God; therefore, I do overcome the world and this is the victory that overcomes the world, even my faith (1 John 5:4).

God the Father has created me worthy of my calling and He is now fulfilling all the good pleasure of His goodness and the work of faith with power that the name of my Lord Jesus Christ is now glorified in me and I am now glorified in Him, according to the grace of our God and the Lord Jesus Christ (2 Thessalonians 1:1, 12).

I am in Christ Jesus and He is in me and in Him dwells all the fullness of the Godhead bodily; I am now complete in Him, who is the head of all principality and power, in whom are hidden all the treasures of wisdom and knowledge (Colossians 2:9-10, 2:3).

It's in You, heavenly Father, that I live and I move and I have my being (Acts 17:28).

The Spirit of truth has come and He is now guiding me into all truth, for He shall not speak of Himself, but whatsoever He shall hear, that He shall speak and He is now showing me and He is now telling me things to come (John 16:13).

As He (Christ Jesus) is, so am I in this world (1 John 4:17).

God the Father chose me in Christ Jesus before the foundation of the world; that I should be holy and without blame before Him in love (Ephesians 1:4).

But of Him I am in Christ Jesus, who of God has been made unto me wisdom, righteousness, sanctification, and redemption. Therefore, I possess the wisdom of God and the mind of Christ (1 Corinthians 1:30).

My love abounds still more and more in knowledge and in all discernment; I approve the things that are excellent; I am sincere and without offense until the day of Christ; I am filled with the fruit of righteousness which are by Jesus Christ to the glory and praise of God (Philippians 1:9-11).

The love of God has been shed abroad in my heart by the Holy Ghost which has been given me; therefore, I choose to walk in love and always forgive everyone (Romans 5:5).

Since the Lord Jesus Christ has become my Lord and Savior, I am no longer a stranger and a foreigner, but I am a fellow citizen with the Saints, and I am a member of the household of God. I (your name) have been built on the foundation of the apostles and the prophets; Jesus Christ Himself being the chief cornerstone (Ephesians 2:19).

I can do all things through Christ who strengthens me (Philippians 4:13).

The Lord is with me and He lets none of my words fall to the ground (1 Samuel 3:19).

Now this is the confidence that I have in You Lord; that if I ask anything according to Your will, You will hear me, and if I know that You hear me, whatever I ask, I know that I have the petitions that I have asked of You (1 John 5:14-15).

For this purpose I have been saved and adopted into the family of God; that I might destroy the works of the devil (1 John 3:8).

God has given me authority to trample on serpents and scorpions and over all the power of the enemy and nothing shall by any means hurt me (John 10:19).

My mind has been, and is continually, being renewed by the Word of God, as a result, I have dominion over every living thing. I prove what is the good and acceptable and perfect will of God (Romans 12:2, Genesis 1:20).

The peace of God, which surpasses all understanding, guards my heart and my mind through Christ Jesus (Philippians 4:17).

With great power, I give witness to the resurrection of the Lord Jesus Christ and great grace is upon me (Acts 4:37).

Because I wait upon the Lord, my strength is renewed, I mount up with wings as an eagle, I run and I am not weary, I walk and I do not faint (Isaiah 40:31).

There is an open heaven over me; the angels of God are ascending and descending upon me (John 1:51).

God is holding my right hand saying to me, "Fear not, I will help you;" therefore, I do not fear (Isaiah 41:13).

The Lord is my light and He is my salvation, whom shall I fear? The Lord is the strength of my life, of whom shall I be afraid? (Psalm 27:1).

A faithful man shall abound in blessings; I am that faithful man (Proverbs 28:20).

I am full of faith and power and I do great wonders and miracles among the people (Acts 6:8).

The Father who is in me, He doeth the works (John 14:10).

POWER SCRIPTURES

"But you shall receive **power** when the Holy Spirit has come upon you; and you shall be witnesses to Me in Jerusalem, and in all Judea and Samaria, and to the end of the earth" (Acts 1:8).

"And when they had set them in the midst, they asked, 'By what **power** or by what name have you done this?'" (Acts 4:7).

"And with great **power the** apostles gave witness to the resurrection of the Lord Jesus. And great grace was upon them all" (Acts 4:33).

"And Stephen, full of faith and **power,** did great wonders and signs among the people" (Acts 6:8).

"The word which God sent to the children of Israel, preaching peace through Jesus Christ—He is Lord of all—that word you know, which was proclaimed throughout all Judea, and began from Galilee after the baptism which John preached: how God anointed Jesus of Nazareth with the Holy Spirit and with **power**, who went about doing good and healing all who were oppressed by the devil, for God was with Him" (Acts 10:36-38).

"For the message of the cross is foolishness to those who are perishing, but to us who are being saved it is the **power** of God" (1 Corinthians 1:18).

"And I, brethren, when I came to you, did not come with excellence of speech or of wisdom declaring to you the testimony of God. For I determined not to know anything among you except Jesus Christ and Him crucified. I was with you in weakness, in fear, and in much trembling. And my speech and my preaching were not with persuasive words of human wisdom, but in demonstration of the Spirit and of **power**, that your faith should not be in the wisdom of men but in the **power** of God" (1 Corinthians 2:1-5).

"For the kingdom of God is not in word but in **power**" (1 Corinthians 4:20).

"For it is the God who commanded light to shine out of darkness, who has shone in our hearts to give the light of the knowledge of the glory of God in the face of Jesus Christ. But we have this treasure in earthen vessels that the excellence of the **power** may be of God and not of us" (2 Corinthians 4:6-7).

"And what is the exceeding greatness of His **power** toward us who believe, according to the working of His mighty **power** which He worked in Christ when He raised Him from the dead and seated Him at His right hand in the heavenly places" (Ephesians 1:19-20).

"Now to Him who is able to do exceedingly abundantly above all that we ask or think, according to the **power** that works in us" (Ephesians 3:20).

"Finally, my brethren, be strong in the Lord and in the **power** of His might" (Ephesians 6:10).

"For our gospel did not come to you in word only, but also in **power,** and in the Holy Spirit and in much assurance, as you know what kind of men we were among you for your sake" (1 Thessalonians 1:5).

"Therefore we also pray always for you that our God would count you worthy of this calling, and fulfill all the good pleasure of His goodness and the work of faith with **power**" (2 Thessalonians 1:11).

"For God has not given us a spirit of fear, but of **power** and of love and of a sound mind" (2 Timothy 1:7).

LORD, THROUGH YOUR COM-
MANDMENTS YOU HAVE MADE
ME WISER THAN MY ENEMIES,
FOR YOUR COMMANDMENTS
ARE EVER WITH ME, I HAVE
MORE UNDERSTANDING THAN
ALL OF MY TEACHERS FOR
YOUR TESTIMONIES ARE MY
MEDITATION.

I UNDERSTAND MORE THAN
THE ANCIENTS BECAUSE I KEEP
YOUR PRECEPTS.

3

TRANSFORMED

Do not be conformed to this world, but be transformed by the renewing of your mind.

(Romans 12:2)

When Jesus raised Lazarus from the dead, the Bible says, "He (Lazarus) came out of the tomb bound hand and foot with grave clothes and his face was wrapped with a cloth. Jesus said to them, 'Loose him and let him go'" (John 11:44). This is a picture of a baby Christian who just got saved. Although he has become a new creation and God sees him as such, he does not know anything about what has just happened to him. That is why the Holy Spirit, through the Apostle Paul, tells us in Romans 12:2, "Do not become conformed to this world, but be transformed by the renewing of your mind."

When you were born into this world, you were born a baby. Your mother had to feed you, wash you, and dress you. You couldn't do anything for yourself until you grew and matured. Then gradually, a little at a time, you began doing things for yourself. It's the same way with the new birth (being born again). When you are first saved, you are born as a spiritual child. Hence, the Apostle Peter said, "as newborn babes" (1 Peter 2:2). However, you are not supposed to stay a babe, you should grow up spiritually.

Most Christians are content with being born again. They do not concern themselves with maturing until something happens to them and then they want to go on a crash program. I have prayed with many Christians when a catastrophe hits them, but most of the time to no avail. You cannot wait until a catastrophe hits to begin to grow spiritually. Begin to grow by God's Word before anything drastic happens to you.

When you first made Jesus the Lord of your life, even though you became a new creation, you didn't look any different and you didn't act differently. Your friends and family recognized who you were just as they did before you got saved. However, once you have been saved for some time, you should look, talk, and act different. The best witness you can give to the Lord Jesus Christ is when someone says, "There is something different about you." What the world is saying about most Christians is, "I have enough problems of my own, why should I change and become like them?"

So how do we become what God intended? First and foremost, we must come into agreement with God. Amos 3:3 says, "Can two walk together, unless they are agreed." The obvious answer is, "No." I have heard Christians say, "I would never say I am righteous." If you have ever said that, you were in disagreement with God. If you have refused to forgive someone, you are in disagreement with God. How can you walk with God and not agree with Him?

Therefore, the first thing you must do to begin this journey, "to be what God intended," is to agree with what God says about you. Even though you don't feel like it, you don't talk like it or even look like it, you still are what God says you are because of Jesus. Once you have come into agreement with God on any given subject, then transformation will begin. Looking back again to Romans 12:2, it tells us that transformation comes with renewing of your mind.

Let's take righteousness as a subject. You know yourself what thoughts have gone through your mind. You know how you acted lately. Therefore, in your mind you think, *You ugly thing you, you are not righteous.* You just disagreed with God.

48

He did not say you are righteous because of what you have done, but He says you are righteous because of Jesus.

Jesus paid the penalty of our sins. He took them upon Himself. "He who knew no sin, was made to be sin that we might become the righteousness of God in Him" (2 Corinthians 5:21). In addition, in Romans 5:17 we are told that righteousness is a free gift. A gift does not have to be earned or paid for; it is a gift because you did nothing for it. However, it must be received. If you were celebrating a birthday and a friend of yours is a noted prankster and he embarrassed you several times before, you might refuse to accept a gift from him. This shows that you can accept or refuse a gift.

So the first thing you must do to become what God intended us to be is to agree with God. The second thing you must do is accept it. You may ask, "How do I do that?" Let me ask you, "How did you receive Jesus as your Lord and Savior?" Romans 10:10 says, "For with the heart one believes unto righteousness and with the mouth confession is made unto salvation." Romans 4:17 says, "As it is written, I have made you a father of many nations, in the presence of him whom he believed, even God, who gives life to the dead and calls those things which do not exist as though they did."

God calls things which do not exist as though they did and He expects us to do the same. All my life I knew that the Bible said, "Beloved now are we the sons of God" (1 John 3:2). But I never did anything about it, and I did not feel that I was a son. One day many years ago during devotions, I came to that realization and I received sonship. I declared, "Father, I see in Your Word that now I am a son of God; You have adopted me into Your family. In Ephesians, you tell me I was predestined before the foundation of the world to adoption as a son of God. Therefore, right now in the name of Jesus I receive adoption by Almighty God, and I declare that I am a son of the most high God."

Nothing changed as far as I was concerned at that moment, but after that day, in my morning prayers, I always gave thanks to God for loving me as He did and for adopting me into His family making me a son. I can't tell you for sure exactly when it happened, but I **know** that I now am a son of God. It became evident through my confession of God's Word. As far as God was concerned, I was always His son, but it did me no good because I didn't **know** it. As I thanked God for sonship, I was renewing my mind. With the renewing of my mind, transformation set in.

Let me give you another example. The Bible tells us that we have been made the righteousness of God in Christ Jesus. God sees it that way and only that way. Yet I know Christians who beg, plead, and cry to God to get Him to do something, but never have their begging, pleading, and crying answered. Why? Their begging proves they have never received righteousness! If they had, they would go boldly to the throne of grace to obtain mercy, grace, and help in their time of need. Therein is the difference; a righteous man knows in the natural he doesn't deserve anything. Jesus, however, deserves everything, and I am righteous because of Him.

**MAKE THE FOLLOWING
CONFESSIONS OUT LOUD FOR
THE GREATEST IMPACT.**

I am a son of the most High God (1 John 3:2).

I have been made righteous by the blood of the Lamb (2 Corinthians 5:21).

I have received abundance of grace and of the gift of righteousness (Romans 5:21).

I have eternal life in me now (John 3:14).

I have and I enjoy God's life, in abundance to the full until it overflows (John 10:10 AMP).

I have the blessing of Abraham upon me (Galatians 3:14).

My body is a temple of the Holy Spirit (1 Corinthians 6:19).

I am just, righteous and holy. Therefore, my path is like the shining sun (Proverbs 4:18).

I am a temple of God; therefore, His Spirit dwells within me (1 Corinthians 3:16).

I praise You Lord, that there is no condemnation to me, for I am in Christ Jesus (Romans 8:1).

I can of myself do nothing, the Father in me, He does the works (John 14:10).

I do not seek my own will, but the will of the Father (John 5:30).

I always do those things that please the Father (John 8:29).

The love of God has been shed abroad in my heart by the Holy Ghost which has been given me; therefore, I walk, act, and talk in and with love (Romans 5:5).

I humble myself under the mighty hand of God, and He is now exalting me – it is nH due time (1 Peter 5:6).

God has given me all things to richly enjoy and that I may share with others (1 Timothy 6:17).

The name of the Lord is a strong tower, I run into it and I am safe (Proverbs 18:10).

For You Father will light my lamp; the Lord God will enlighten my path (Psalm 18:28).

I am more than a conqueror through Jesus Christ, my Lord and my Savior; God always causes me to triumph in Christ (2 Corinthians 2:14; Romans 8:37).

God will be with me, He will not fail nor forsake me; therefore, I am strong and very courageous (1 Samuel 41:10).

Be it unto me according to Your Word, Lord (Luke 1:38).

My help comes from the Lord, who made heaven and earth (Psalm 121:1).

The Lord has delivered me from every evil work and He will preserve me for His Heavenly Kingdom (Psalm 140:1).

God goes with me, therefore, I am distinguished from all other peoples, for I am the people of God (Exodus 33:16).

Because I am the sheep of Your pasture, I do hear and I do know Your voice, and You do speak to me continually (John 10:14).

I am in the Kingdom of God. He reigns, He rules, and I am under His Authority. Jesus Christ is Lord over my life and I bow to His Lordship. In the Name of Jesus, I resign as Lord over my life, Jesus you are my Lord, I am Yours.

I am wonderfully well and blessed, and I am highly favored of the Lord. Because I am the seed of Abraham,

his blessing is on my life. Therefore, I am blessed and I am a blessing to others.

All of the gifts of the Spirit function in my life and ministry as needed; they are free to operate in me. You are the God of breakthrough; therefore, breakthrough has come to my house, my life, and my ministry.

Father, I commit my day into Your care; Your will be done in my life today.

TRANSFORMATION SCRIPTURES

"And do not be conformed to this world, but be transformed by the renewing of your mind, that you may prove what is that good and acceptable and perfect will of God" (Romans 12:2).

"But we all, with unveiled face, beholding as in a mirror the glory of the Lord, are being transformed into the same image from glory to glory, just as by the Spirit of the Lord" (2 Corinthians 3:18).

"Therefore we do not lose heart. Even though our outward man is perishing, yet the inward man is being renewed day by day" (2 Corinthians 4:16).

"But you have not so learned Christ, if indeed you have heard Him and have been taught by Him, as the truth is in Jesus: that you put off, concerning your former conduct, the old man which grows corrupt according to the deceitful lusts, and be renewed in the spirit of your mind, and that you put on the new man which was created according to God, in true righteousness and holiness" (Ephesians 4:20-24).

"Do not lie to one another, since you have put off the old man with his deeds, and have put on the new man who is renewed in knowledge according to the image of Him who created him, where there is neither Greek nor Jew, circumcised nor uncircumcised, barbarian, Scythian, slave nor free, but Christ is all and in all" (Colossians 3:9-11).

"For if by the one man's offense death reigned through the one, much more those who receive abundance of grace and of the gift of righteousness will reign in life through the One, Jesus Christ" (Romans 5:17).

"Be of the same mind toward one another. Do not set your mind on high things, but associate with the humble. Do not be wise in your own opinion. Repay no one evil for evil. Have regard for good things in the sight of all men. If it is possible, as much as depends on you, live peaceably with all men" (Romans 12:16-18).

"Now may the God of patience and comfort grant you to be like-minded toward one another, according to Christ Jesus, that you may with one mind and one mouth glorify the God and Father of our Lord Jesus Christ. Therefore receive one another, just as Christ also received us, to the glory of God" (Romans 15:5-7).

I AM NO LONGER
CONFORMED TO THIS
WORLD, BUT I CHOOSE
TO BE TRANSFORMED
BY THE RENEWING OF
MY MIND THAT I MAY
BE ABLE TO PROVE
WHAT IS THAT GOOD,
AND ACCEPTABLE, AND
PERFECT WILL OF GOD.

4

PRAYER

Pray without ceasing.

(1 Thessalonians 5:17)

To pray in its simplest form is to talk to God. However, there is a difference between "talking to" and "talking at." "Talking to" is a two-way street; both parties have something to say. Don't you just love it when you are with someone who dominates the conversation and you can't get one word in. I wonder how God feels when we do this to Him? That is what I call "talking at." "Talking to" is stopping to hear what the other person has to say.

We have already been told to, "Seek first the Kingdom of God and His righteousness and all these things shall be added to you" (Matthew 6:33). Notice He said **all things**; God wants you to have things. Things are okay. In Hebrews 11:1 we are told, "Faith is the substance of things;" things are in God's plan. But we should not be going after things. He said, "Seek first the Kingdom of God and His righteousness," then He goes on to say, "Things will be added to you." But what do we do? Most Christians are constantly asking God for things, instead of seeking Him first.

This is not a study on the Kingdom of God, however, I can tell you that if God reigns, He rules, and has complete authority over your life; you are in the Kingdom. So how do we get to that place? We get there by seeking after God, His Kingdom, and His righteousness. What does that look like? The Bible tells us that we have become the righteousness of God in Christ Jesus. God sees us as righteous, but do we see ourselves that way.? Mostly no; positionally we have been made righteous, but many Christians do not experience it because they have not accepted it as an accomplished fact.

You do this first by agreeing with God about what His Word says and then by confessing it until it becomes real in you. "Be not deceived, God is not mocked; whatever you sow that is what you will reap" (Galatians 6:7). If you sow to your mind "I am so unworthy," that is what you will experience. If you sow, "Thank you Father, you have made me righteous in Christ Jesus," you will eventually begin to experience it. You will no longer beg God for your needs, but you will go boldly to His Throne of Grace and you will find mercy in the time of need.

My focus on prayer has become a little different since I now believe all of the Word of God. I totally believe what the Word says about me as a child of God. I completely accept what the Bible says that Jesus accomplished in His birth, His life, His sacrifice on the cross, and His resurrection on my behalf. Starting with the fact that He became sin for me so that I might be made the righteousness of God in Him, I accept what He says about me is the only real truth. The great exchange is the greatest wonder in all of the world. Imagine God died in my place so that I could live! Therefore, I choose to honor God by totally believing what His Word says about me.

As a result, my prayer is not focused on me and my needs because He meets all of my needs according to His riches in glory by Christ Jesus. Instead my focus is centered on becoming all that God has planned for me before the foundation of the world. Remember, we have been adopted into the family of God. We are now **sons** of God. Therefore, I search the Scriptures to find out what I am supposed to be and I pray that first. Let me give you an example.

Proverbs 2:1 says, "My son, if you receive My Words, and treasure My Commands within you, so that you incline your ear to wisdom, and apply your heart to understanding; yes, if you cry out for discernment and lift up your voice for understanding; if you seek her as silver and search for her as for hidden treasures; then, you will understand the fear of the Lord, and find the Knowledge of God."

So this is what I pray, "Father, I receive Your Word, and I treasure Your Commands within me. I incline my ear to wisdom, and I apply my heart to understanding. I do cry out for discernment, Father, and I lift up my voice for understanding. I seek for her as silver and search for her as for hidden treasure. Because of it, I do understand the fear of the Lord and I am now finding the Knowledge of God." That is better than constantly asking God for mundane things. Remember, seek ye first the Kingdom of God and His righteousness and all these **things** will be added to you.

In Ephesians 1:4 we are told that God chose us in Christ Jesus before the foundation of the world, that we should be holy and without blame before Him in love. There was a time in my life that if you asked me if I was holy, I would answer absolutely not. But, that has changed, I did absolutely nothing to become holy. God has graced me as holy, therefore, I humble myself under the mighty hand of God and I agree with Him that I have been made Holy.

My confession is, "Father, I see in Your Word that You chose me in Christ Jesus before the foundation of the world, that I should be holy and without blame before you in love. I receive it by faith and I declare that I have been made Holy because of Jesus. Thank You Lord."

The truth of the matter is that because of what Jesus has done for me, I can now stand before God, man, and the devil just as if I had never sinned! To some that might seem presumptuous on my part, and to others that might almost be sacrilegious. However, to a student of the Word of God, that should be the norm so study to show thyself approved unto God.

Following is a guide on how to pray:

Father, I receive Your Word and treasure Your commands within me. I incline my ear to wisdom and I apply my heart to understanding. I do cry out for discernment. Father, I lift up my voice for understanding. I seek for her as silver and search for her as for hidden treasure. Because of it, I do understand the fear of the Lord and I am now finding the Knowledge of God (Proverbs 2:1-5).

I thank you Father, that You are directing my steps by Your Word Lord, and You allow no iniquity to have dominion over me (Psalm 119:33).

Thank You Father, that You have set a watch before my mouth and You Lord keep the door of my lips (Psalm 141:3).

I thank You Father, that the words of my mouth and the meditations of my heart are acceptable in Thy sight oh Lord, my strength and my redeemer (Psalm 19:14).

Thank You Lord, that you keep changing my perception as needed because of it, I perceive Your Word as You do.

Lord, I am the sheep of Your pasture, I do hear Your voice. I do recognize it and I follow You and only You do I follow (John 10:4, 14, 27).

I am calling upon You Lord, and You will answer me, and You will show me great and mighty things which I have not known (Jeremiah 29:11).

Lord, I thank You that with all boldness, I speak Your Word and You stretch out Your hand to heal, and that signs and wonders are done through the name of Your Holy Servant Jesus (Acts 4:29-30).

Father, let me know You always; that I may know You (Exodus 33:13).

Father, I pray that doors of utterance be opened for me, and that I may open my mouth boldly to make known the mystery of the gospel (Ephesians 6:19).

Father, I pray that You will direct my heart into the love of God, and into the patience of Christ (2 Thessalonians 3:5).

One morning while I was praying and spending time with the Lord, this thought came to me. Jesus said, "Most assuredly, I say to you, he who believes in Me, the works that I do, he will do also; and greater works than these he will do because I go to my Father" (John 14:12). Perhaps it might be a good thing if I looked to see how He did them. After all we are told to be imitators of God, so I decided to do just that. I began a thorough search of the four Gospels to see, "How did Jesus do it?" After much study, to my astonishment I realized that Jesus did not pray for the sick. Instead, He gave commands. The following are some of the commands that I found.

"Arise take up your bed, and go to your house" (Matthew 9:6).

"I am willing be cleansed" (Mark 1:41).

"Stretch out your hand" (Mark 3:5).

"Peace be still" (Mark 4:39).

"Little girl I say to you arise" (Mark 6:41).

"Be opened" (Mark 7:34).

"Be quiet, and come out of him" (Luke 4:35).

"Woman, thou art loosed of thine infirmities" (Luke 13:12).

"Receive your sight" (Luke 18:42).

"Young man, I say to you arise" (Luke 7:14).

"Go your way, your son lives" (John 4:50).

"Rise, take up your bed and walk" (John 5:8).

"Lazarus, come forth" (John 11:43).

Since doing this research, I no longer pray for people to be healed. Instead, I give commands. There are some things that I feel compelled to keep reminding you, lest you get the wrong impression. It's the Father in me, He does the works. I am just a conduit of His grace and His love. Once I stopped praying and asking God to do what He has already done by just speaking a command, I have had many more healings and miracles take place in my ministry.

At His ascension into heaven, one of the many things that Jesus said was, "They will lay hands on the sick and they will recover." He did not say pray for the sick. Many people praying for the sick spend time asking God to do what Jesus has already done, instead of receiving what has been already accomplished by His death, burial, and resurrection.

Jesus said, "All authority has been given to me, both in heaven and on earth." Then He gave the charge, "Go into all the world," thereby transferring His authority to "whosoever will."

PRAYING TO THE HOLY SPIRIT

It is the job of the Holy Spirit to teach, to lead us into all truth, and to tell us things to come. You must address the Holy Spirit to be taught by Him. He is a part of the Trinity, which makes up the Godhead. Jesus said, "But the Helper, the Holy Spirit, whom the Father will send in My name, He will teach you all things" (John 14:26). Again He said, "He will guide you into all truth; for He will not speak on His own authority, but whatever He hears He will speak: and He will tell you things to come. He will glorify Me, for He will take what is mine and declare it to you" (John 16:13-14). Therefore, ask the Holy Spirit for these things:

1. Teach me Holy Spirit, "the fear of the Lord."

2. Teach me Holy Spirit, "to do good."

3. Teach me Holy Spirit, "to worship God in spirit and in truth."

4. Teach me Holy Spirit, "how to delight myself in the Lord."

5. Teach me Holy Spirit, "how to rejoice in the Lord."

6. Teach me Holy Spirit, "about my inheritance."

7. Teach me Holy Spirit, "how to minister to the Lord."

8. Teach me Holy Spirit, "to seek first the Kingdom of God and His righteousness."

9. Holy Spirit, I want to have an encounter with You, fill me to overflowing.

As you ask the Holy Spirit for these things, they will become a reality in your life. The Bible says, "You have not because you ask not!" Ask that your joy may be full. Jesus said, "Until now you have asked nothing in My name; ask, and you will receive, that your joy may be full" (John 16:24).

In John 17 Jesus Prayed:

1. That we may have the full measure of His joy in us (verse 13).

2. That we would be kept from the evil one (verse 15).

3. That we would be sanctified (verse 17).

4. That we would be one in God the Father and the Son (verse 21).

5. That we would have His glory in and upon us (verse 22).

6. That we would experience His presence (verse 23).

7. That we would have God's love in us (verse 26).

Therefore, based on these scriptures, make the following **Declarations of Faith**. Job 22:28 says, "You will also declare a thing and it will be established for you."

1. I declare that I (your name) have the full measure of His joy in me.

2. I declare that I (your name) am kept from the evil one.

3. I declare that I (your name) have been sanctified by the blood of the Lamb.

4. I declare that I (your name) am one with God the Father and God the Son.

5. I declare that I (your name) have the glory of the Lord in and upon me.

6. I declare that I (your name) experience His presence.

7. I declare that I (your name) have God's love in me.

I declare this by faith in Your Word Lord, and it is becoming a reality in me. Thank You, Lord.

Keep this thought in mind that Jesus always got His prayers answered; therefore, I can claim what He prayed for as present reality in my life.

PRAYER SCRIPTURES

"But I say to you, love your enemies, bless those who curse you, do good to those who hate you, and pray for those who spitefully use you and persecute you" (Mathew 5:44).

"But you, when you pray, go into your room, and when you have shut your door, pray to your Father who is in the secret place; and your Father who sees in secret will reward you openly" (Matthew 6:6).

"Therefore pray the Lord of the harvest to send out laborers into His harvest" (Matthew 9:38).

"Watch and pray, lest you enter into temptation. The spirit indeed is willing, but the flesh is weak" (Matthew 26:41 and Mark 14:38).

"Therefore I say to you, whatever things you ask when you pray, believe that you receive them, and you will have them" (Mark 11:24).

"Likewise the Spirit also helps in our weaknesses. For we do not know what we should pray for as we ought, but the Spirit Himself makes intercession for us with groanings which cannot be uttered" (Romans 8:26).

"Rejoice always, pray without ceasing, in everything give thanks; for this is the will of God in Christ Jesus for you" (1 Thessalonians 5:16-18).

"I desire therefore that the men pray everywhere, lifting up holy hands, without wrath and doubting" (Timothy 2:8).

"Confess your trespasses to one another, and pray for one another, that you may be healed. The effective, fervent prayer of a righteous man avails much" (James 5:16).

The Lord Has Blessed Me

And He Keeps Me.

The Lord Has Made His

Face To Shine Upon Me.

The Lord Is Gracious

Towards Me.

The Lord Continually

Gives Me Peace.

Amen

5

I AM

Before Abraham was, I AM.

(John 8:58)

When Moses asked God, "Whom shall I say has sent me? What shall I say to them?" God responded, "I AM who I AM." He said, "Thus shall you say to the children of Israel, 'I AM has sent me to you'" (Exodus 3:14). When the Jews said to Jesus, "You are not yet fifty years old and have you seen Abraham?" Jesus answered them saying, "Most assuredly I say to you, before Abraham was, I AM" (John 8:57-58).

You will notice that both God the Father and God the Son spoke of themselves only in the present tense, not the past or the future. The mistake that we as Christians have been making is that we seem to be stuck mostly in the future tense. We need to get out of that mode and like the Father and the Son, we need to get into the present. Calling things which be not as though they are is putting things into the present time, **now**. The Bible says, "Beloved, **now** are we the Sons of GOD" (1 John 3:2 emphasis added). We are expecting "to become," not confessing that we "are **now**."

The following "I AM" confessions will help you take what is rightfully yours **now** and allow them to become real to you. Remember, we have been told in Romans 12:2, "Do not be conformed to this world, **but** become transformed by the renewing of your mind" (emphasis added). Why do we do this? So that we may be able to prove the good, acceptable, and perfect will of God.

As you make these "I AM" confessions, you will be renewing your mind. Next, you will begin to think differently about yourself, and you will eventually begin to act differently. Remember, without faith it is impossible to please God (Hebrews 11:6). Therefore, make these "I AM" confessions in faith. Do not stumble at what you are presently experiencing, but focus on the fact that God already sees you in this way. This is one of the meanings of "humble yourself under the mighty hand of God, that He may exalt you in due time" (1 Peter 5:6). You may think, *I presently do not see myself as these confessions declare, but I am humbling myself and saying of myself what God already thinks about me.* You can sing all you want, "be glorified," but singing those words does not glorify God. "By this is my Father **glorified**, that you bear much fruit; so you will be my disciples" (John 15:8 emphasis added). These confessions will eventually produce a harvest in your life, thereby producing fruit in your life which will bring glory to God.

Remember that saying, "Everything is going to be alright," is a future tense confession. It will always remain in the future and will never be a present truth reality until you change it from future tense to present tense. You do this by confessing "everything is alright **now**!" Everything may not seem alright when you first start saying it, but do not be deceived, God is not mocked, whatever you sow that is what you will reap (Galatians 6:7).

I AM CONFESSIONS

I am an AMBASSADOR of God.

I am ABRAHAM's seed.

I am ABOVE and not beneath.

I am ACCEPTED in the beloved.

I am ADOPTED into God's family.

I am ALIVE unto God.

I am ALIVE unto righteousness.

I am ALIVE together with Christ.

I am AS Jesus is in the world.

I am a BELIEVER.

I am BLESSED.

I am the BELOVED of God.

I am BLAMELESS before God.

I am a BLESSOR.

I am the BODY OF CHRIST.

I and the BRANCH – HE is the VINE.

I am BRINGING God pleasure.

I am BURIED with Christ.

I am CALLED to liberty.

I am CALLED of God.

I am a CHILD of the King.

I am in CHRIST JESUS.

I am a CHOSEN man.

I am a CITIZEN of Heaven.

I am CROWNED with glory.

I am CLOTHED with compassion.

I am a CO-LABORER with God.

I am COMPLETE in Him.

I am a CONDUIT of the glory of God.

I am a CONQUEROR.

I am CONTINUALLY being cleansed of sin.

I am in COVENANT with God.

I am CRUCIFIED with Christ.

I am DEAD to sin.

I am DEARLY loved by God.

I am DELIVERED out of the power of darkness.

I am DESTINED for good works.

I am DIVINELY transported by God.

I am a DOER of God's Word.

I am EATING the good of the land.

I am the EYES, HANDS, and FEET of Jesus.

I am the ELECT of God.

I am ENCOUNTERING His love.

I am EVERYTHING God's Word says I am.

I am EXPERIENCING His presence.

I am FAITHFUL.

I am FAR from oppression.

I am FEARLESS.

I am FEARFULLY and wonderfully made.

I am FILLED with the fruit of RIGHTEOUSNESS.

I am FILLED with God.

I am FILLED with JOY.

I am FILLED with KNOWLEDGE.

I am FILLED with LOVE.

I am FILLED with PEACE.

I am FILLED with WISDOM.

I am FILLED with GLORY.

I am FREE from CARE.

I am FREE from CONDEMNATION.

I am FREE from STRIFE.

I am FREE from UNFORGIVENESS.

I am FORGIVEN.

I am FULL of FAITH.

I am FURNISHED in ABUNDANCE.

I am a GIVER.

I am GLAD.

I am GLORIFIED.

I am GOOD.

I am a HABITATION of God.

I am the HEAD and not the tail.

I am HEALED.

I am an HEIR according to the promise.

I am HIGHLY favored of God.

I am HUMBLE.

I am HOLY.

I am INCREASING in God's knowledge.

I am an IMITATOR of God.

I am an INSTRUMENT of God's mercy.

I am JOYFUL.

I am JUSTIFIED.

I am KEPT by God.

I am KIND.

I am a KING in life.

I am the LENDER not the borrower.

I am LIGHT.

I am LOVED by God.

I am LONG-SUFFERING.

I am MEEK.

I am a MEMBER of His Body.

I am a NEW creation in Christ.

I am an OVERCOMER.

I am PATIENT.

I am at PEACE.

I am PEACEFUL.

I am the PEOPLE of God.

I am PLEASING to God.

I am a PRIEST.

I am PROTECTED.

I am PROSPEROUS.

I am PURSUING God.

I am a REAPER.

I am REDEEMED.

I am a REFLECTION of the Lord.

I am RICH.

I am the RIGHTEOUSNESS of God.

I am ROOTED and grounded in love.

I am a SAINT of God.

I am SANCTIFIED.

I am SAVED.

I am SEALED with the Holy Spirit of promise.

I am SEATED in Heavenly Places.

I am the SHEEP of His pasture.

I am a SIGNS, WONDERS, and MIRACLES man.

I am SINCERE.

I am a SON of Light

I am a SON of God.

I am a SOWER.

I am a SOUL winner.

I am a SPECIMEN of perfect health.

I am STANDING on God's promises.

I am STRENGTHENED with all might.

I am STRONG.

I am SURROUNDED with God's favor.

I am a TEMPLE of the Holy Spirit.

I am a TITHER.

I am in UNION with God.

I am VICTORIOUS.

I am WALKING In the Spirit.

I am WAXED strong in the Spirit.

I am WELL.

I am WALKING in divine favor with God.

I am WILLING and OBEDIENT.

I am WISER than my enemies

I am WITHOUT sin.

I am WITHOUT offense.

I am WONDERFULLY well.

I am His WORKMANSHIP.

These "I Have Been" confessions will help you become transformed. They will renew your mind to what **has already been** done by our Savior and Lord.

I have been made ACCEPTED in the beloved.

I have been ADOPTED.

I have been made ALIVE.

I have been BAPTIZED.

I have been BLESSED.

I have been BUILT for a habitation of God in the Spirit.

I have been BUILT on the foundation of the apostles and the prophets; Jesus Christ Himself being the Chief Cornerstone.

I have been CREATED in Christ Jesus.

I have been made a CITIZEN of heaven.

I have been CLEANSED by His Blood.

I have been CONFORMED to the image of God's Son.

I have been made a CONQUEROR.

I have been DELIVERED.

I have been made to have DOMINION over all the works of God's hand.

I have been FORGIVEN.

I have been HEALED.

I have been made HOLY.

I have been made a KING.

I have been made LIGHT in the LORD.

I have been made a MEMBER of His Body.

I have been made a MEMBER of the household of God.

I have been made a PRIEST.

I have been RAISED up together with Christ.

I have been REDEEMED.

I have been RESTORED.

I have been made RICH.

I have been made RIGHTEOUS.

I have been SANCTIFIED.

I have been made to be SEATED in Christ Jesus.

I have been SET FREE.

I have been made a SON.

I have been TRANSLATED.

I have been made His WORKMANSHIP.

I ENDURE LONG, I AM PATIENT
AND I AM KIND.

I AM NEVER ENVIOUS NOR DO I EVER
BOIL OVER WITH JEALOUSY.

I AM NOT BOASTFUL OR VAINGLORIOUS.

I DO NOT DISPLAY MYSELF HAUGHTILY.

I AM NOT CONCEITED.

I AM NOT ARROGANT.

I AM NOT RUDE, AND I DO NOT ACT
UNBECOMINGLY.

I DO NOT INSIST ON MY OWN RIGHTS
OR MY OWN WAY.

I AM NOT SELF-SEEKING.

I AM NOT TOUCHY.

I AM NOT FRETFUL OR RESENTFUL.

I TAKE NO ACCOUNT OF AN EVIL
DONE TO ME.

I PAY NO ATTENTION TO A SUFFERED WRONG.

I DO NOT REJOICE AT INJUSTICE.

I DO REJOICE WHEN RIGHT AND
TRUTH PREVAIL.

I BEAR UP UNDER ANYTHING AND
EVERYTHING THAT COMES.

I AM EVER READY TO BELIEVE THE
BEST OF EVERY PERSON.

MY HOPES ARE FADELESS UNDER
ALL CIRCUMSTANCES.

I ENDURE EVERYTHING
WITHOUT WEAKENING.

I NEVER FAIL.

I NEVER FADE OUT.

I NEVER BECOME OBSOLETE,
AND I NEVER COME TO AN END.

(1 Corinthians 13:4-8 AMP)

6

Healing

He sent His Word and healed them.

(Psalm 107:20)

The Bible explicitly teaches us that the Lord Jesus Christ not only bore all of our sins and iniquities, but also took upon Himself every sickness, every disease, and all infirmities. Isaiah, looking forward to the cross declared, "By His stripes we **are** healed" (Isaiah 53:5). Peter, looking back at the cross declared, "By Whose stripes ye **were** healed" (1 Peter 2:24). Isaiah said, "are" but Peter said, "were" making our healing past tense. When something is past tense that means it has already happened. We need to have our minds renewed to the fact that our healing has already occurred. We are not waiting for it to happen.

Once again let me remind you of the three scriptural references for the basis of this book:

1.   Jesus said, "You can have what you say."
2.   We believe, therefore, we speak what we believe.
3.   We call things which be not as if they were.

We never deny that we are sick. If you are sick that happens to be a **fact**; however, that is not the **truth**. The only **truth** that exists in the universe is God's Word. So we always turn to God's Word to see what the **truth** is concerning any matter.

So let's see what the truth is:

"He sent His word and healed them, and delivered them from their destructions" (Psalm 107:20).

"Surely He has borne our griefs and carried our sorrows; yet we esteemed Him stricken, Smitten by God, and afflicted. But He was wounded for our transgressions, He was bruised for our iniquities; the chastisement for our peace was upon Him, and by His stripes we are healed" (Isaiah 53:4-5).

"Who Himself bore our sins in His own body on the tree, that we, having died to sins, might live for righteousness—by whose stripes you were healed" (1 Peter 2:24).

"When evening had come, they brought to Him many who were demon-possessed. And He cast out the spirits with a word, and healed all who were sick, that it might be fulfilled which was spoken by Isaiah the prophet, saying: **'He himself took our infirmities and bore our sicknesses.'**" (Matthew 8:16-17 emphasis added).

You will notice that in Psalm 107:20 "**sent**" is past tense, He already did that. In Isaiah 53:4-5 it says, "He **was** wounded," past tense; "He **was** bruised," past tense. In 1 Peter 2:24, "**were** healed," past tense; and in Matthew 8:16-17, "He Himself **took** our infirmities and He **bore** our sicknesses." **He took and He bore**, both are in the past tense. Everything that Jesus did for us has been done in the past; therefore, it is now an accomplished fact—**past tense**.

Since this is all **truth,** we never ask God to do for us what He has already done. Instead, we thank Him for what He has done and accept it in faith. The following healing confession is put in the past tense. Remember when you say, "Everything is **going to be** alright," you are putting "alright" into the **future**. However, if you say, "Everything is alright **now**," it is present tense. You are now calling the thing that is not as if it is now. You will also notice in the Healing Confession that you are not asking God to do anything. Instead, you are claiming for yourself what God has said.

1. Now this is the confidence that I have in You Lord, that if I ask anything according to Your will, You will hear me. Since I know You hear me, whatever I ask, I know that I have the petitions that I am asking of You.
2. I know that it is Your will to heal me because You have said in Your Word, that You sent Your Word and healed them.
3. Your Word also tells me that Jesus healed them all, that it might be fulfilled which was spoken by Isaiah the Prophet, "He Himself took our infirmities and He bore our sicknesses."
4. Then it says in Your Word, "He Himself bore our sins in His own Body on the tree that we, being dead to sins, should live unto righteousness by whose stripes we were healed."
5. Therefore, I am coming boldly to Your Throne of Grace that I may obtain mercy and I might find grace to help in my time of need.

I declare and I decree in the name of my Lord Jesus Christ, that I am now healed, from the crown of my head to the soles of my feet. Jesus Himself took my infirmities and bore my sickness so that I would not have to. Therefore, I refuse to bear what Jesus bore for me. **By His stripes I am now healed!**

HEALING CONFESSION

FATHER, in the name of the Lord Jesus,

By the Blood of the Lamb, and

on the authority of Your Holy Written Word,

I thank You Lord for You have sent Your Word

and You have healed me.

You have delivered me from all destruction.

Thank You Father, that the Lord Jesus Christ Himself,

He took all of my infirmities and He bore all of my sicknesses;

by His stripes I am now healed and made whole.

I am the redeemed of the Lord,

Whom the Lord has redeemed out of the hands of the enemy. by His precious blood

No weapon formed against me can prosper, and

every tongue that rises up against me I now condemn.

My righteousness is from You, Oh GOD.

Greater is He who is in me than he who is in the world.

Father, You have removed sickness from my midst.

I have been redeemed from the curse of the law.

I have been delivered out of the power of darkness.

I have been translated into the Kingdom of the Son of Your love.

I have been set free, therefore I am free indeed.

I boldly say, "I am free, I am free, I am free!"

I bless You Lord and all that is within me blesses Your Holy Name.

I will never forget all of Your benefits.

You have forgiven all of my iniquities.

You have healed ALL of my diseases.

You have blessed my bread.

You have blessed my water.

You have removed sickness from my midst.

There shall be no evil before me

nor shall any plague come near my dwelling.

I wait upon You Lord and You do renew my strength.

I can boldly say, "I am strong, I am strong, I am strong!"

The law of the Spirit of Life in Christ Jesus

has made me free from the Law of Sin and Death.

You Father, are watching over Your Word to perform it.

I dwell in Your secret place, FATHER.

I abide under Your shadow.

I say of You, "Lord, You are my refuge,

You are my fortress, You are my God.

In You and only in You do I trust."

You have delivered me from every entrapment

that the enemy has designed against me

because of You and Your love for me.

I am not afraid of evil reports.

I am not afraid of life and its environment.

A thousand may fall at my side,

ten thousand at my right hand, but

I shall remain standing, untouched, and unharmed.

You have given Your Angels charge over me.

They do keep me in all my ways.

They do keep me from mishap, incident, and accident.

I can boldly say, "I am now divinely transported by GOD."

When I sleep my sleep is sweet.

GOD gives me, His Beloved sweet sleep.

When I call upon You, You do answer me.

You are with me in trouble.

Should I go through fire, I shall not burn

neither will my clothes smell of smoke.

Should I go through the waters, I shall not drown

You, my FATHER, will always deliver me.

Since God is for me

no one can be against me.

With long life You will satisfy me.

You will show me Your salvation

in the Name of the Lord Jesus Christ.

I thank You for all of this, FATHER.

I give praises to Your Wonderful and Holy Name.

I give You the glory in Jesus Name, Amen.

HEALING SCRIPTURES

"So he cried out to the LORD, and the LORD showed him a tree. When he cast it into the waters, the waters were made sweet. There He made a statute and an ordinance for them, and there He tested them, and said, 'If you diligently heed the voice of the LORD your God and do what is right in His sight, give ear to His commandments and keep all His statutes, I will put none of the diseases on you which I have brought on the Egyptians. For I am the LORD who heals you'" (Exodus 15:25-26).

"So you shall serve the LORD your God, and He will bless your bread and your water. And I will take sickness away from the midst of you" (Exodus 23:25).

"He sent His word and healed them, and delivered them from their destructions" (Psalm 107:20).

"Bless the LORD, O my soul, and forget not all His benefits: who forgives all your iniquities, Who heals all your diseases, who redeems your life from destruction, Who crowns you with loving-kindness and tender mercies, who satisfies your mouth with good things, so that your youth is renewed like the eagle's" (Psalm 103:2-5).

"A merry heart does good, like medicine, but a broken spirit dries the bones" (Proverbs 17:22).

"He is despised and rejected by men, a Man of sorrows and acquainted with grief. And we hid, as it were, our faces from Him; He was despised, and we did not esteem Him. Surely He has borne our griefs and carried our sorrows; yet we esteemed Him stricken, smitten by God, and afflicted. But He was wounded for our transgressions, He was bruised for our iniquities; the chastisement for our peace was upon Him, and by His stripes we are healed" (Isaiah 53:3-5).

"When evening had come, they brought to Him many who were demon-possessed. And He cast out the spirits with a word, and healed all who were sick, that it might be fulfilled which was spoken by Isaiah the prophet, saying: '**He himself took our infirmities and bore our sicknesses**'" (Matthew 8:16-17 emphasis added).

"And behold, a leper came and worshiped Him, saying, 'Lord, if You are willing, You can make me clean.' Then Jesus put out His hand and touched him, saying, 'I am willing; be cleansed.' Immediately his leprosy was cleansed" (Matthew 8:2-3).

"Behold, I give you the authority to trample on serpents and scorpions, and over all the power of the enemy, and nothing shall by any means hurt you" (Luke 10:19).

"Christ has redeemed us from the curse of the law, having become a curse for us (for it is written, '**Cursed is everyone who hangs on a tree**'), that the blessing of Abraham might come upon the Gentiles in Christ Jesus, that we might receive the promise of the Spirit through faith" (Galatians 3:13-14).

"Therefore submit to God. Resist the devil and he will flee from you" (James 4:7).

"Who Himself bore our sins in His own body on the tree, that we, having died to sins, might live for righteousness—by whose stripes you were healed" (1 Peter 2:24).

"He who sins is of the devil, for the devil has sinned from the beginning. For this purpose the Son of God was manifested, that He might destroy the works of the devil" (1 John 3:8).

"Beloved, I pray that you may prosper in all things and be in health, just as your soul prospers" (3 John 1:2).

YOU LORD ARE MY ROCK.

YOU ARE MY FORTRESS.

YOU ARE MY GOD.

YOU ARE MY STRENGTH.

IN YOU AND ONLY IN YOU

DO I TRUST.

YOU ARE MY BUCKLER.

YOU ARE THE HORN OF

MY SALVATION.

YOU ARE MY HIGH TOWER.

I DO CALL UPON YOU, LORD.

YOU ARE WORTHY TO

BE PRAISED.

THEREFORE, I WILL BE SAVED

FROM MY ENEMIES.

7

PROSPERITY

For you know the grace of our Lord Jesus Christ,
that though He was rich, yet for your sakes
He became poor, that you through
His poverty might become rich.

(2 Corinthians 8:9)

The word salvation implies the idea of safety, soundness, deliverance, preservation, and healing. God intends the whole man to experience salvation. In 1 Thessalonians 5:23 it says, "Now may the God of peace Himself sanctify you completely: and may your whole spirit, soul, and body be preserved blameless at the coming of the Lord Jesus Christ." In 3 John 2 it states, "Beloved, I pray that you may prosper in all things and be in health just as your soul prospers." The mistake that many Christians make is they isolate promises of God to one area only; not allowing it to encompass the whole man. Therefore, if you confess, "I am blessed, God's Word says so," appropriate that to your entire being not just one area.

However, there are portions of Scripture that explicitly tell us the subject that is being talked about. Two such verses are found in 2 Corinthians 8 and 9 where it would be dishonest to say He is not referring to money. In 2 Corinthians 8:9 we read, "For you know the grace of our Lord Jesus Christ that, though He was rich, yet for your sakes He became poor, that you through His poverty might become rich." This is part and parcel of the great exchange.

1. He became sin so we might become righteous.
2. He died so we might live.
3. He went to hell so we could go to heaven.
4. He became poor so we might be rich.

Many Christians struggle financially only due to their not getting God's revelation on sowing and reaping. After Noah's flood, God said in Genesis 8:22, "While the earth remains, seed time and harvest, and cold and heat, and winter and summer, and day and night shall not cease." The only area that we are encouraged to prove God by His holy written Word is in the area of finances. God says, "Prove Me now in this, says the Lord of Hosts" (Malachi 3:10b).

In keeping with the theme of this book, I want to give you scriptures to use over your giving. I am not necessarily speaking of tithing. I believe every Christian should be or should become a hilarious giver. Ask God to show you where or to whom you should plant a seed and how much the seed should be; remembering always that the Word of God is the seed. On the next page, register your gift and make those confessions over it every day and watch God's faithfulness.

Amount_____Name_____

Amount_____Name_____

Amount_____Name_____

Amount_____Name_____

Amount_____Name_____

Father, I am standing on Your Word that declares: "Give and it shall be given unto you good measure, pressed down, shaken together and running over shall men put into my bosom" (Luke 6:36).

Your Word says: "The Kingdom of God is as if a man should scatter seed on the ground and should sleep by night and rise by day; and the seed should sprout and grow; he himself does not know how. For the earth yields crops by itself: First the blade then the head; after that the full grain in the head. But, when the grain ripens, immediately he puts in the sickle because the harvest has come" (Mark 4:26-29).

It is also written in Your Word: "Now, he who supplies seed to the sower, and bread for food will supply and multiply the seed that I have sown and increase the fruit of my righteousness" (2 Corinthians 9:10).

It is also written in Your Word Father: "Because I have a bountiful eye, I am blessed for I give my bread to the poor" (Proverbs 22:9).

Again Your Word says: "I have and will continually cast my bread upon the waters and I shall and will continually find it after many days" (Ecclesiastes 11:1).

Before we turn to the next three pages and make the confessions on them, let me remind you that Abraham called himself, and told others to call him, "Father of Many Nations." The Holy Spirit, through the Apostle Paul, said, "Call those things which do not exist as though they did" (Romans 4:17b).

You will be doing the same with the following confessions:

Father, in the name of the Lord Jesus Christ of Nazareth, the Son of the most high God, by the Blood of the Lamb and on the authority of the Holy written Word of God, I thank You that Satan has restored to me sevenfold, all that he has ever stolen from me according to Your Holy written Word.

Thank You Father, that the wealth of the sinner, that has been stored up for the just, has been poured into my bosom.

I thank you Father, that Your angels have gathered hidden treasures in secret places and they have brought them to me.

I thank you Father, that because I am a tither, you have the Windows of Heaven opened unto me, you have poured out a blessing on me that there is not room enough to contain it, and You rebuke the devour for my sake.

I thank you Father, that because I have given it is given unto me, good measure pressed down, shaken together, and running over men have given into my bosom.

With faith in Your Word, I have received some thirty, some sixty or some one hundredfold.

I shout for joy my Lord and I am glad; I favor Your righteous cause my Lord and I will continually say, "Let the Lord be magnified," for You Lord take pleasure in my prosperity.

Father, I believe that I require no aid or support, and that I am furnished in abundance for every good work and charitable donation.

You have given me all things to richly enjoy and that I may share with others.

I have been blessed with every spiritual blessing in the heavenly places in Christ Jesus.

I am blessed in the store; I am blessed in the basket; I am blessed going in; I am blessed going out.

I am above and not beneath; I am the head and not the tail.

I am the lender and not the borrower.

I delight myself in You Lord, and You have given me the desires of my heart.

Because I am willing and obedient, I am now eating the good of the land.

You have supplied all of my needs according to Your riches in glory by Christ Jesus.

Because I seek you Lord, I do not want any good thing.

I am a good man; therefore, I am leaving an inheritance to my children's children.

I remember You Lord daily for you are the One who gives me power to get wealth.

Jesus, You came in order that I may have and enjoy life in abundance to the full until it overflows.

Thank you Father that while the earth remains, seed time and harvest shall not cease.

I have planted; I will continue to plant.

I am now cultivating; I will continue to cultivate.

I am now reaping my harvest and I will continue to reap.

Thank You, Father for blessing me; thank You for Your prosperity.

Thank You, Father that Abraham's blessing are upon me now.

Now, ministering spirits of God, you that heed to the voice of God's Word; you ministers of Him, who do His good pleasure:

I charge you, in the name of the Lord Jesus Christ of Nazareth, Son of the most high God, see to it that Satan continues to restore to me, sevenfold, all that he has ever stolen from me.

See to it that the wealth of the sinner that has been stored up for the just is continually being poured into my bosom.

Continue to gather hidden riches of secret places and bring them to me.

Continue to gather my harvest; some thirty, some sixty and some one hundredfold, and bring it to me.

Father, You have commanded blessings on me in my storehouses, and all that I have set my hands to. You have blessed me in the land that You have given me. I am using it to be a blessing to others and I am using it to finance the gospel. I receive all of these by faith in the name of the Lord Jesus Christ of Nazareth.

PROSPERITY SCRIPTURES

"And you shall remember the LORD your God, for it is He who gives you power to get wealth that He may establish His covenant which He swore to your fathers, as it is this day " (Deuteronomy 8:18).

Now it shall come to pass, if you diligently obey the voice of the LORD your God, to observe carefully all His commandments which I command you today, that the LORD your God will set you high above all nations of the earth.

And all these blessings shall come upon you and over-take you, because you obey the voice of the LORD your God: Blessed shall you be in the city, and blessed shall you be in the country. Blessed shall be the fruit of your body, the produce of your ground and the increase of your herds, the increase of your cattle and the offspring of your flocks. Blessed shall be your basket and your kneading bowl. Blessed shall you be when you come in, and blessed shall you be when you go out.

The LORD will cause your enemies who rise against you to be defeated before your face; they shall come out against you one way and flee before you seven ways.

The LORD will command the blessing on you in your storehouses and in all to which you set your hand, and He will bless you in the land which the LORD your God is giving you.

The LORD will establish you as a holy people to Himself, just as He has sworn to you, if you keep the commandments of the LORD your God and walk in His ways. Then all peoples of the earth shall see that you are called by the name of the LORD, and they shall be afraid of you.

And the LORD will grant you plenty of goods, in the fruit of your body, in the increase of your livestock, and in the produce of your ground, in the land of which the LORD swore to your fathers to give you. The LORD will open to you His good treasure, the heavens, to give the rain to your land in its season, and to bless all the work of your hand. You shall lend too many nations, but you shall not borrow.

And the LORD will make you the head and not the tail; you shall be above only, and not be beneath, if you heed the commandments of the LORD your God, which I command you today, and are careful to observe them. So you shall not turn aside from any of the words which I command you this day, to the right or the left, to go after other gods to serve them. (Deuteronomy 28:1-14)

"In the morning sow your seed, and in the evening do not withhold your hand; for you do not know which will prosper, either this or that, or whether both alike will be good" (Ecclesiastes 11:6).

"See, I have set before you today life and good, death and evil, in that I command you today to love the LORD your God, to walk in His ways, and to keep His commandments, His statutes, and His judgments, that you may live and multiply; and the LORD your God will bless you in the land which you go to possess" (Deuteronomy 30:15-16).

"The young lions lack and suffer hunger; but those who seek the LORD shall not lack any good thing" (Psalm 34:10).

"Honor the LORD with your possessions and with the firstfruits of all your increase; so your barns will be filled with plenty, and your vats will overflow with new wine" (Proverbs 3:9-10).

"Let them shout for joy and be glad, who favor my righteous cause; and let them say continually, 'Let the LORD be magnified, who has pleasure in the prosperity of His servant'" (Psalm 35:27).

"The blessing of the LORD makes one rich, and He adds no sorrow with it " (Proverbs 10:22)

"He will bless those who fear the LORD, both small and great. May the LORD give you increase more and more, you and your children. May you be blessed by the LORD, who made heaven and earth" (Psalm 115:13-15).

"By humility and the fear of the LORD are riches and honor and life" (Proverbs 22:4).

"Do not lay up for yourselves treasures on earth, where moth and rust destroy and where thieves break in and steal; but lay up for yourselves treasures in heaven, where neither moth nor rust destroys and where thieves do not break in and steal. For where your treasure is, there your heart will be also" (Mathew 6:19-21).

"For you know the grace of our Lord Jesus Christ, that though He was rich, yet for your sakes He became poor, that you through His poverty might become rich" (2 Corinthians 8:9).

"Give, and it will be given to you: good measure, pressed down, shaken together, and running over will be put into your bosom. For with the same measure that you use, it will be measured back to you" (Luke 6:38).

"Beloved, I pray that you may prosper in all things and be in health, just as your soul prospers" (3 John 1:2).

GOD IS ABLE TO MAKE

ALL GRACE ABOUND

TOWARD ME, THAT I,

ALWAYS HAVING ALL

SUFFICIENCY IN ALL

THINGS, MAY HAVE

ABUNDANCE FOR EVERY

GOOD WORK

(2 Corinthians 9:8).

8

ALL

ALL Authority has been given me.
(Matthew 28:18)

He Healed ALL who were sick.
(Matthew 8:16)

He will Teach you ALL things.
(John 14:26)

He will Guide you into ALL Truth.
(John 16:13)

There is a saying that goes like this, "What is it about the word 'no' that you don't understand." I want to pose a different question to you; what is it about the word **all** that you don't understand? We have a habit of minimizing words in the Bible, but maximizing words in the newspaper. Allow me to bring light on this subject. Words have the same meaning, whether you see it in the newspaper or in your Bible. Therefore, "no" in your Bible is the same as "no" in the newspaper. It is opposite of "yes!"

At His Ascension, Jesus told those who had assembled there, "**All** authority has been given to me in heaven and on earth. Go therefore, and make disciples of all nations, baptizing them in the Name of the Father and of the Son and of the Holy Spirit" (Matthew 28:18-19). **Question:** Since He has been given **all** authority, does anyone else have any? The answer to that question is an absolute "No!" He, the Lord Jesus Christ, has been given "**All** authority" and "a Name that is above every name" (Philippians 2:9). In Colossians 2:15 it says He, "Disarmed principality and powers." He stripped satan of the armor that he trusted in, "He made a public spectacle of them, and He triumphed over them in it."

I asked the Lord once, "Exactly what was the armor that satan trusted in?" The answer to that question is found in Luke 4:5-7, "Then the devil, taking Him up on a high mountain, showed Him all the Kingdoms of the world in a moment of time. The devil said to Him, 'All this authority I will give you and their glory; for this has been delivered to me and I give it to whomever I wish. Therefore, if You will worship before me, all will be Yours." Therein lay his strength. What he said to Jesus at that moment was true. Had it not been true, then it would not have been a temptation. The Word of God calls it a temptation.

By His death, burial and resurrection, Jesus stripped the devil of that authority and regained it for all of humanity. All of humanity can access it after accepting what Jesus accomplished for them. Thus Jesus, after having defeated satan, stripping him of that armor and authority given him by Adam, could now say, "**All** authority has been given to Me." **All** means "**All.**" We as believers need to receive a revelation of this. The first words Jesus said recorded in Matthew's Gospel, apart from what He said to the devil in the wilderness were, "Repent, for the Kingdom of Heaven is at hand" (Matthew 4:17).

Have you ever noticed that Jesus said, "At hand," not "has come"? It was because the Kingdom could not be here for us until Jesus took it away from satan. That is what 1 Corinthians 2:8 reveals to us, "None of the rulers of this age knew; for had they known, they would not have crucified the Lord of Glory." They thought that they had defeated Him. Little did they know that they had played right into Jesus' hands. It reminds me of the Trojan horse. Jesus willingly, of Himself, laid down His life as a final sacrifice on the altar of God. He gave Himself freely for all of the sins of mankind.

After Jesus declared to His disciples that He had been given **all** authority, He went on to say, "Go therefore," thereby transferring the authority that He had received to whosoever will. Authority is transferrable; Jesus did this to His twelve disciples in Luke 9:1-2, then to the seventy in Luke 10:1-16.

However, in verse nine He says, "Heal the sick who are there, and say to them, the Kingdom of God has come near to you." I believe that they were able to operate out of the Kingdom of God on credit. What I mean by that is, they were not yet born again and Jesus had not stripped satan of the armor, but they operated in the Kingdom of God anyway. Today we should be operating and ordering our lives out of and from the Kingdom of God. "For the kingdom of God is not food and drink, but righteousness and peace and joy in the Holy Spirit" (Romans 14:17).

Now I want to present an entirely different aspect of the word "**all**." When I prayed for the sick, not everyone would receive their healing. As a result, I had many different excuses as to why they did not receive. I read a book once where the author believed for a certain percentage of those in the auditorium to be healed. All of my life I'd heard other ministers make excuses for everyone not receiving their healing. It is sad many of us if not all of us, at least some of the time, mimic and/or repeat what we hear other ministers say. Sometimes we don't process what we hear; we just repeat without giving it much or any thought. I was guilty of that!

One day, while meditating on the excuses that had been made, this thought came to me. Jesus said, "The Father who dwells in Me does the works" (John 14:10). That instantly liberated me from excuses because I saw myself as the delivery boy for God and nothing else. My job is to believe what Jesus said and to do it in faith. However, there is something we must see. Jesus said, "Most assuredly, I say to you, he who believes in Me, the works that I do he will do also" (John 14:12). My question to you is this: What are the works that Jesus did? Well, He turned water into wine; He healed the sick; He cast out demons, and He raised the dead, to mention some of the things He did.

The thing that I want you to see where healing is concerned is this: Whenever Jesus healed people, as in many, as opposed to healing an individual, we are told, "He healed them **all**" (Matthew 12:15). "And healed them **all**" (Luke 6:19). "He healed **every** sickness and **every** disease among the people" (Matthew 9:35). So why have we not been believing that everyone, "**all**" would be healed? Do we see ourselves as God sees us? Do we understand and know who and what we have become in Christ Jesus? Have we received **all** that has been purchased for us by His blood? One of the things that I have no tolerance for is a spirit of poverty on a born again Christian. It is not only a natural condition, it is a spiritual condition also. The Bible says, "Awake to righteousness and do not sin; for some do not have the knowledge of God" (1 Corinthians 15:34). It is time that we awaken to what we have become and what we have been made.

It is time to start believing God that "**all**" will be healed. The anointing of Almighty God is upon us. We are to reign in this life as kings through the righteousness of our Lord and our Savior Christ Jesus. Do not allow the world to put you in its mold. Become "transformed by the renewing of your mind." It is something you do every day. Confess good words over yourself and contend for the faith. Peter said in his Epistle that we have received precious faith, the same faith he had. We need to develop it and use it.

Make the Following confession:

Father, Jesus said, "The works that I do shall you do also." Your Word declares over and over that Jesus healed them ALL. Jesus also said, "The Father in Me, He does the works." Father, You are in Me just as You were in Jesus during His earthly ministry. Therefore, by the Blood of the Lamb and on the authority of Your Holy Written Word, I believe that ALL will be healed in my life and

ministry. After all Father, You are the healer. I am just the delivery boy, so I expect ALL to be healed.

This is not presumption on my part, instead it is called: "Have the Faith of God." We, as the Body of Christ, need to begin to believe **all** of the Word of God; not pick and choose!

Now let me show you some other "**all**" things from the Word of God. "But the Helper, the Holy Spirit, whom the Father will send in My Name, He will teach you **all** things" (John 14:26). Then He says, "He will guide you into **all** truth; for He will not speak on His own authority, but whatever He hears He will speak; He will tell you things to come" (John 16:13-14).

1. He will Teach you "**all**" Things.
2. He will Guide you into "**all**" Truth.

God is limited by what we believe. Remember, Jesus could do no mighty works in Nazareth. He marveled at their unbelief. We need to take the limit off of God and begin to start believing "**all**" that the Bible says we have become and "**all**" that we can do.

Meditate on these scriptures until they begin to transform you. They will indeed change the way you think:

"But seek first the kingdom of God and His righteousness, and **all** these things shall be added to you" (Matthew 6:33).

"But Jesus looked at them and said to them, 'With men this is impossible, but with God **all** things are possible'" (Matthew 19:26).

"And whatever things you ask in prayer, believing, you will receive" (Matthew 21:22).

"Jesus said to him, 'If you can believe, **all** things are possible to him who believes'" (Mark 9:23).

"But Jesus looked at them and said, 'With men it is impossible, but not with God; for with God **all** things are possible'" (Mark 10:27).

"Behold, I give you the authority to trample on serpents and scorpions, and over **all** the power of the enemy, and nothing shall by any means hurt you" (Luke 10:19).

"But seek the kingdom of God, and **all** these things shall be added to you" (Luke 12:31).

"Now, Lord, look on their threats, and grant to Your servants that with **all** boldness they may speak Your Word" (Acts 4:29).

"How God anointed Jesus of Nazareth with the Holy Spirit and with Power, who went about doing good and healing **all** who were oppressed by the devil, for God was with Him" (Acts 10:38).

"Yet in **all** these things we are more than conquerors through Him who loved us" (Romans 8:37).

"For **all** the promises of God in Him are Yes, and in Him Amen, to the glory of God through us" (2 Corinthians 1:20).

"And God is able to make **all** grace abound toward you, that you, always having **all** sufficiency in all things, may have an abundance for every good work" (2 Corinthians 9:8).

"For you are **all** sons of God through faith in Christ Jesus" (Galatians 3:26).

"To know the love of Christ which passes knowledge; that you may be filled with **all** the fullness of God. Now to Him who is able to do exceedingly abundantly above **all** that we ask or think, according to the power that works in us" (Ephesians 3:19-20).

"And my God shall supply **all** your need according to His riches in glory by Christ Jesus" (Philippians 4:19).

"That you may walk worthy of the Lord, fully pleasing Him, being fruitful in **every** good work and increasing in the knowledge of God" (Colossians 1:10).

"And you are complete in Him, who is the head of **all** principality and power" (Colossians 2:10).

"You are **all** sons of light and sons of the day. We are not of the night nor of darkness" (1 Thessalonians 5:5).

"Test **all** things; hold fast what is good" (1 Thessalonians 5:21).

"Meditate on these things; give yourself entirely to them, that your progress may be evident to **all**" (1 Timothy 4:15).

"Then His fame went throughout **all** Syria; and they brought to Him **all** sick people who were afflicted with various diseases and torments, and those who were demon-possessed, epileptics, and paralytics; and He healed them" (Matthew 4:24).

"When evening had come, they brought to Him many who were demon-possessed. And He cast out the spirits with a word, and healed **all** who were sick, that it might be fulfilled which was spoken by Isaiah the prophet, saying: **'He himself took our infirmities and bore our sicknesses'''** (Matthew 8:16-17).

"But when Jesus knew it, He withdrew from there. And great multitudes followed Him, and He healed them **all**" (Matthew 12:15).

"When the sun was setting, **all** those who had any that were sick with various diseases brought them to Him; and He laid His hands on **every** one of them and healed them" (Luke 4:40).

"And He came down with them and stood on a level place with a crowd of His disciples and a great multitude of people from all Judea and Jerusalem, and from the seacoast of Tyre and Sidon, who came to hear Him and be healed of their diseases, as well as those who were tormented with unclean spirits. And they were healed. And the whole multitude sought to touch Him, for power went out from Him and healed them **all**" (Luke 6:17-19).

"Then Jesus went about all the cities and villages, teaching in their synagogues, preaching the gospel of the kingdom, and healing **every** sickness and **every** disease among the people" (Matthew 9:35).

"And when He had called His twelve disciples to Him, He gave them power over unclean spirits, to cast them out, and to heal **all** kinds of sickness and **all** kinds of disease" (Matthew 10:1).

"Jesus departed from there, skirted the Sea of Galilee, and went up on the mountain and sat down there. Then great multitudes came to Him, having with them the lame, blind, mute, maimed, and many others; and they laid them down at Jesus' feet, and He healed them. So the multitude marveled when they saw the mute speaking, the maimed made whole, the lame walking, and the blind seeing; and they glorified the God of Israel" (Mathew 15:29-31).

9

OFFENDED

Blessed is he who shall not be offended in me.

(Matthew 11:6)

When the Disciples of John the Baptist came to Jesus asking, "Are You the Coming One, or do we look for another?" Jesus responded by saying, "Go and tell John that which you hear and see. The blind receive their sight and the lame walk, the lepers are cleansed and the deaf hear; the dead are raised up and the poor have the Gospel preached to them." Then He said a very astounding thing, "And blessed is he who is not offended because of Me." Why would anyone be offended by what He was doing? Why was it necessary for Jesus to make that statement?

I am not sure that I have the complete picture on this, however, I do know this. As far as Satan and his demons are concerned, you can have your timed, well-choreographed, all done decent and in order, do not offend anybody Sunday morning meeting as long as the "Spirit" does not manifest Himself. After all there may be people with other beliefs present. However, when the "Spirit of the Lord is present to heal," those demons become agitated and they try to do all they can to stop the move of the Holy Spirit. But they must get authority from a man. To get that authority they must get someone to become offended by what is happening.

The most religious people in the day that Jesus was manifest on this earth were the very same people that got offended by what Jesus was doing. They should have been the ones pointing others to Jesus. They should have been the ones supporting the claim that He was indeed the Son of God. Instead, they became offended. Things haven't changed much today. It is the most religious people who get offended by the move of the Holy Spirit and by the manifestation of God's Power.

What most Christians have to come to grips with is that Christianity is not a religion; instead, it is a family. God the Father has become our Father and Jesus Christ has by choice become our Elder Brother and the Head of His Body here on earth. We have become sons and daughters of the Most High God. God is love, therefore, we have become love, and we love all that God does. We do not easily become offended.

If you have become offended by anything found in this book, that is not you who is offended but the enemy trying to steal the Word that has been sown in your heart. Instead of receiving that offense by agreeing with the thought, cast it out in Jesus Name; remembering all the time that it is all the Word of God.

In Mark 4:11, we are told, "To you it has been given to know the mystery of the Kingdom of God." Instead of accepting an offence, ask God to reveal to you personally the mystery of the Kingdom of God.

Jesus said in Mark 4:26-29, "So is the Kingdom of God, as if a man should cast seed into the ground: and should sleep, and rise night and day, and the seed should spring and grow up, he knoweth not how. For the earth bringeth forth fruit of herself; first the blade then the ear, after that, the full corn in the ear. But, when the fruit is brought forth, immediately, he putteth in the sickle because the harvest has come." Words are seeds. Inherent in every Word of God is the ability for that Word to produce what it says.

As you keep speaking (confessing) God's Word day in and day out, things will begin to take place in your life, you know not how. But you will grow stronger and stronger and things that bothered you before will no longer affect you. Keep at it, don't quit, God's Word works, but you must work it. You have to speak it out of your mouth for it to come to pass.

This is my prayer for you:

In the Name of the Lord Jesus Christ, I pray for everyone who has read this book. I pray that you will overcome offenses and that you will become all that God has already planned that you should be. That you will become strong in the Lord and in the power of His might. That you will get a revelation of who you really have become and what you truly are. I pray that the Word of God will begin to work mightily in you. That you will abound in all and every grace, exceedingly and abundantly above all that you can ask or even think. I pray that you will become God-minded and begin to recognize the leading of the Holy Spirit in your life. I pray that you will begin to put God's Word first place in your life, above all other things. Amen.

OFFENDED SCRIPTURES

"Yet he has no root in himself, but endures only for a while. For when tribulation or persecution arises because of the word, immediately he stumbles" (Matthew 13:21).

"So they were offended at Him. But Jesus said to them, 'A prophet is not without honor except in his own country and in his own house'" (Matthew 13:57).

"Then His disciples came and said to Him, 'Do You know that the Pharisees were offended when they heard this saying?'" (Matthew 15:12).

"And then many will be offended, will betray one another, and will hate one another" (Matthew 24:10).

"Then Jesus said to them, 'All of you will be made to stumble because of Me this night, for it is written: "I will strike the shepherd and the sheep of the flock will be scattered" ' " (Matthew 26:31).

"Peter answered and said to Him, 'Even if all are made to stumble because of You, I will never be made to stumble'" (Matthew 26:33).

"And they have no root in themselves, and so endure only for a time. Afterward, when tribulation or persecution arises for the word's sake, immediately they stumble" (Mark 4:17).

"'Is this not the carpenter, the Son of Mary, and brother of James, Joses, Judas, and Simon? And are not His sisters here with us?' So they were offended at Him" (Mark 6:3).

"Peter said to Him, 'Even if all are made to stumble, yet I will not be'" (Mark 14:29).

"And blessed is he who is not offended because of Me" (Luke 7:23).

"These things I have spoken to you that you should not be made to stumble" (John 16:1).

PEACE BE UNTO ME;

PEACE BE TO

MY HOUSE;

PEACE BE TO ALL

THAT I HAVE.

(1 Samuel 25:6)

I would be pleased to hear from you if this book has had an effect on your life.

You may order additional copies of this book by contacting me at:

November thru May

John Franco
465 Riviera Blvd West
Naples, Florida 34112
239-692-9784

June thru October

John Franco
4 Heywood Court
Brick, New Jersey 08724
732-903-6209

CPSIA information can be obtained at www.ICGtesting.com
Printed in the USA
LVOW12s1037080714

393234LV00002B/2/P